Mikella makes reading the Bible not only enjoyable but also less overwhelming and easier to understand. This book will help you dive deeper into reading and studying the Bible to grow closer to God and truly change your life. If you want to dig into God's Word but you don't know where to start, this book is for you.

ASHLEY HETHERINGTON, author and founder of The Honey Scoop

We all chase after something. None of us are immune from the human desire to find purpose, meaning, and sacredness in this life. Mikella compassionately and faithfully reminds readers that we are most ourselves and will be most fulfilled when we open the pages of God's Word.

AMY GANNETT, author and founder of Tiny Theologians and The Bible Study Schoolhouse

Chasing Sacred not only emphasizes the necessity of humility in approaching the Bible but also ignites a passion for knowing God's Word on a deeper level. It provides practical guidance for seeking the whole character of God and chasing after His sacred truths. Through its wisdom, readers will find themselves not only hungry for God's Word but equipped with the practical tools to nourish that hunger, ultimately fostering a more profound connection with Him. I appreciate Mikella's stories and the way she approaches God's Word with joy, prayer, and gratitude so we can know more of God's true character.

STEFANIE ROUSE, relationship mentor, digital creator, and author

In *Chasing Sacred*, Mikella is honest, relatable, and real. She doesn't just tell you to read God's Word; she shows you how to fall in love with God's Word. This book will arm you with practical tools to implement in your Bible study, while also keeping you engaged, entertained, and laughing along the way.

TARA SUN, author of *Surrender Your*
with Tara podcast

Full of practical tools and Mikella's heartfelt encouragement, *Chasing Sacred* will help you not only read and understand God's Word but also truly love and live by it. This soul-stirring guide encourages you to do more than just study; it invites you to immerse yourself in the transformative power of God's truth.

MICHELLE MYERS, cohost of the *She Works His Way* podcast; author of the Conversational Commentary series, *She Works His Way*, and *Famous in Heaven and at Home*

There is no more excellent endeavor for the Christian than knowing God through understanding His Word. Sadly, we are experiencing perhaps the worst epidemic of biblical illiteracy in modern history. Yet God still ignites His people to seek Him by chasing an understanding of His sacred Word. In doing so, He also blesses the church with teachers who can equip and encourage the church toward spiritual maturity. This is why I'm thankful for Mikella Van Dyke's book *Chasing Sacred*. More than simply a "Bible study book," Mikella brings us along on a guided tour of her own life, experiences, and personal discovery of Inductive Bible Study. Not only is Mikella a skilled writer, she is also a gracious hostess, carefully and kindly walking the reader through the timeless principles of hermeneutics. I warmly recommend this helpful book!

NATE PICKOWICZ, pastor of Harvest Bible Church in Gilmanton Iron Works, New Hampshire, and author of *How to Eat Your Bible*

Chasing Sacred is an incredible book that helps readers learn how to establish themselves in God's Word in a way where the Bible becomes real and transformative to each one of us. It empowers the reader with invaluable tools to understand Scripture and builds a strong foundation for how to read the Bible without needing to rely on other people's interpretations. Whether you've been reading the Bible for five minutes or fifty years, *Chasing Sacred* reminds readers how the Word of God comes alive and how we can each grow closer to our heavenly Father by understanding His Word.

ABIGAIL ROBERTSON, CBN News correspondent

Learning how to correctly interpret and read the Bible is one of the most important things we can do as Christians. *Chasing Sacred* beautifully leads you step by step in a non-overwhelming way to study Scripture for what it is truly saying rather than what we want it to say. This is a must-read for anyone looking to dive deeper in their Bible study, and your mind will be blown at how astonishing the Bible truly is!

ALLYSON GOLDEN, founder of Words Are Golden and author of *Arise and Shine*

Many Christians know they need to get serious about studying the Bible but are often too intimidated or overwhelmed to know where to start! This book is just the right resource to meet this need. Mikella approaches the topic with warmth and wisdom, putting the daunted reader immediately at ease as she presents the process of Inductive Bible Study in plain and accessible language. With the right knowledge and tools, anyone can study the Bible, and this book will give you the confidence to make it happen!

NAOMI VACARO, author of *Quiet* and founder of Wholehearted

Mikella's love for God, His Word, and teaching theology is deeply refreshing. As Christians, our need to know what we believe and why we believe what we believe is crucial. The stories and teachings that fill these pages paint a beautiful reminder of this truth for us that you are sure to be encouraged in and challenged by. This book undoubtedly puts the Father's glory on full display.

ELLE CARDEL, founder of Daughter of Delight

The way in which Mikella can help a person understand Scripture and deepen their relationship with the Lord is unlike anything I've ever experienced. She has a spirit about her that meets you where you are and points you to Jesus. What you will learn and be able to apply to your daily walk after reading these pages is going to break barriers and change families.

HOPE REAGAN HARRIS, author of *Purpose Doesn't Pause*

Mikella is the kind of Bible teacher all of us need! She knows the Bible deeply, both through academic study and personal experience, but she leads with humility and grace. This book is the perfect place to start if you're looking to go deeper in your understanding of how to study Scripture, but more than that, this book is the perfect place to start if you want to experience the transformative power of submitting your life to the truth of God's Word.

WHITNEY LOWE, founder of Scribble Devos

Chasing Sacred is the valuable resource you need if you are seeking a richer understanding of the Bible. In a world filled with lies and deception, we need this more than ever. With clarity and depth, Mikella guides you with practical tools and spiritual wisdom that will lead you to better understand Scripture, why it matters, and the importance of sharing it with others. You will be returning to this book as a reference for years to come.

ASHLEY MORGAN JACKSON, bestselling author of *Tired of Trying*; speaker and writer for Proverbs 31 Ministries

Journey into the heart of Scripture with *Chasing Sacred* by Mikella. Her words thread together a rich tapestry of insights, illuminating the profound depths of the Bible. Through a skillful road map, Mikella empowers readers to see the text in insightful ways, inviting a thoughtful exploration of God's Word. You will continue returning to these thoughtful and biblically based words over and over.

BETHNY RICKS, author, speaker, and leadership expert

Mikella has written a book this generation needs. What are we all chasing? What do our hearts yearn for? *Chasing Sacred* is a road map for our hearts as we learn to seek after God with all our being, falling in love with His Word and heart again. We need this message.

ALEXANDRA HOOVER, speaker, Bible teacher, and author of *Eyes Up* and *Without Wavering*

In a world confused about truth, Mikella breaks down how to study the Bible to know the truth *and be set free*. After you close *Chasing Sacred*, things like Bible charting, the metanarrative, and word studies will actually make sense. Not to mention you'll know the ins and outs of translation philosophies, genres, and the context of what you're reading in the Bible! You won't just know, but as she drives home, you'll be a doer of the Word. Trust me when I say you'll never study the Bible the same again!

HEIDI LEE ANDERSON, author of *P.S. It's Gonna Be Good* and social media personality @heidileeanderson

CHASING SACRED

...s and sisters in Christ. May God our Father give you grace and peace. 3 We always ...nd we give thanks to God, the Father of our Lord Jesus Christ. 4 For we have heard ... in Christ Jesus and your love for all of God's people, 5 which come from your confid... at God has reserved for you in heaven. You have had this expectation ever since you ... the truth of the Good News. 6 This same Good News that came to you is going out all ... It is bearing fruit everywhere by changing lives, just as it changed your lives fro... rst heard and understood the truth about God's wonderful grace. 7 You learned abou... from Epaphras, our beloved co-worker. He is Christ's faithful servant, and he is he... ir behalf. 8 He has told us about the love for others that the Holy Spirit has given ...ve not stopped praying for you since we first heard about you. We ask God to give yo... edge of his will and to give you spiritual wisdom and understanding. 10 Then the w... ill always honor and please the Lord, and your lives will produce every kind of go... e while, you will grow as you learn to know God better and better. 11 We also pray t... e strengthened with all his glorious power so you will have all the endurance and ...ed. May you be filled with joy, 12 always thanking the Father. He has enabled you ... inheritance that belongs to his people, who live in the light. 13 For he has rescue... ngdom of darkness and transferred us into the Kingdom of his dear Son, 14 who pur... m and forgave our sins. 15 Christ is the visible image of the invisible God. He exis... ing was created and is supreme over all creation, 16 for through him God created ev... heavenly realms and on earth. He made the things we can see and the things we can ... s thrones, kingdoms, rulers, and authorities in the unseen world. Everything was ... th him and for him. 17 He existed before anything else, and he holds all creation to... is also the head of the church, which is his body. He is the beginning, supreme ov... rom the dead. So he is first in everything. 19 For God in all his fullness was pleas... st, 20 and through him God reconciled everything to himself. He made peace with... ven and on earth by means of Christ's blood on the cross. 21 This includes you who ... ay from God. You were his enemies, separated from him by your evil thoughts and ac... now he has reconciled you to himself through the death of Christ in his physical ... lt, he has brought you into his own presence, and you are holy and blameless as you ... m without a single fault. 23 But you must continue to believe this truth and sta... Don't drift away from the assurance you received when you heard the Good News. Th... as been preached all over the world, and I, Paul, have been appointed as God's serv... im it. 24 I am glad when I suffer for you in my body, for I am participating in the su... st that continue for his body, the church. 25 God has given me the responsibility of ... urch by proclaiming his entire message to you. 26 This message was kept secret for ... nerations past, but now it has been revealed to God's people. 27 For God wanted the... e riches and glory of Christ are for you Gentiles, too. And this is the secret: Chris... This gives you assurance of sharing his glory. 28 So we tell others about Christ, w

CHASING SACRED

*Learn How to Study Scripture to Pursue God
and Find Hope in Him*

MIKELLA VAN DYKE

TYNDALE
MOMENTUM®

A Tyndale nonfiction imprint

Visit Tyndale online at tyndale.com.

Visit the author online at chasingsacred.com.

Tyndale, Tyndale's quill logo, *Tyndale Momentum*, and the Tyndale Momentum logo are registered trademarks of Tyndale House Ministries. Tyndale Momentum is a nonfiction imprint of Tyndale House Publishers, Carol Stream, Illinois.

Chasing Sacred: Learn How to Study Scripture to Pursue God and Find Hope in Him

Copyright © 2024 by Mikella Van Dyke. All rights reserved.

Cover photograph of clouds by Dominik Schröder on Unsplash.com.

Author photo by Celia O'Brien, copyright © 2023. All rights reserved.

Interior illustrations of speech bubbles copyright © by IconPacks. All rights reserved.

Designed by Julie Chen

Published in association with the literary agency of Books & Such Literary Management, 52 Mission Circle, Suite 122, PMB 170, Santa Rosa, CA 95409.

All Scripture quotations, unless otherwise indicated, are taken from the Holy Bible, *New International Version,*® *NIV.*® Copyright © 1973, 1978, 1984, 2011 by Biblica, Inc.® Used by permission. All rights reserved worldwide.

Scripture quotations marked BSB are taken from The Holy Bible, Berean Standard Bible, BSB. Copyright © 2016, 2018 by Bible Hub. Used by permission. All rights reserved worldwide.

Scripture quotations marked ESV are from The ESV® Bible (The Holy Bible, English Standard Version®), copyright © 2001 by Crossway, a publishing ministry of Good News Publishers. Used by permission. All rights reserved.

Scripture quotations marked GNT are taken from the Good News Translation in Today's English Version, Second Edition, copyright © 1992 by American Bible Society. Used by permission.

Scripture quotations marked KJV are taken from the *Holy Bible*, King James Version.

Scripture quotations marked NKJV are taken from the New King James Version,® copyright © 1982 by Thomas Nelson. Used by permission. All rights reserved.

Scripture quotations marked NASB are taken from the (NASB®) New American Standard Bible,® copyright © 1960, 1971, 1977, 1995 by The Lockman Foundation. Used by permission. All rights reserved. www.lockman.org.

Scripture quotations marked NLT are taken from the *Holy Bible*, New Living Translation, copyright © 1996, 2004, 2015 by Tyndale House Foundation. Used by permission of Tyndale House Publishers, Carol Stream, Illinois 60188. All rights reserved.

Scripture quotations marked NRSV are taken from the New Revised Standard Version Bible, copyright © 1989 National Council of the Churches of Christ in the United States of America. Used by permission. All rights reserved worldwide.

Scripture quotations marked NET are taken from the New English Translation, NET Bible,® copyright ©1996–2006 by Biblical Studies Press, L.L.C. http://netbible.com. All rights reserved.

For information about special discounts for bulk purchases, please contact Tyndale House Publishers at csresponse@tyndale.com, or call 1-800-323-9400.

Library of Congress Cataloging-in-Publication Data

A catalog record for this book is available from the Library of Congress.

ISBN 978-1-4964-8071-2

Printed in the United States of America

30	29	28	27	26	25	24
7	6	5	4	3	2	1

To my parents,
who taught me how to love.
Thanks for always believing in me.

nd we give thanks to God, the Father of our Lord Jesus Christ. 4 For we have heard
in Christ Jesus and your love for all of God's people, 5 which come from your confid
t God has reserved for you in heaven. You have had this expectation ever since you
the truth of the Good News. 6 This same Good News that came to you is going out
It is bearing fruit everywhere by changing lives, just as it changed your lives fro
rst heard and understood the truth about God's wonderful grace. 7 You learned abo
from Epaphras, our beloved co-worker. He is Christ's faithful servant, and he is he
r behalf. 8 He has told us about the love for others that the Holy Spirit has given
e not stopped praying for you since we first heard about you. We ask God to give yo
edge of His will and to give you spiritual wisdom and understanding. 10 Then the w
ll always honor and please the Lord, and your lives will produce every kind of go
e while, you will grow as you learn to know God better and better. 11 We also pray t
e strengthened with all His glorious power so you will have all the endurance and
ed. May you be filled with joy, 12 always thanking the Father. He has enabled you
inheritance that belongs to his people, who live in the light. 13 For he has rescue
ngdom of darkness and transferred us into the Kingdom of his dear Son, 14 who purc
m and forgave our sins. 15 Christ is the visible image of the invisible God. He exis
ing was created and is supreme over all creation, 16 for through Him God created ev
heavenly realms and on earth. He made the things we can see and the things we can
s thrones, kingdoms, rulers, and authorities in the unseen world. Everything was c
h Him and for Him. 17 He existed before anything else, and He holds all creation to
is also the head of the church, which is His body. He is the beginning, supreme ov
om the dead. So He is first in everything. 19 For God in all His fullness was pleas
st, 20 and through Him God reconciled everything to himself. He made peace with
ven and on earth by means of Christ's blood on the cross. 21 This includes you who
ay from God. You were His enemies, separated from him by your evil thoughts and ac
now he has reconciled you to himself through the death of Christ in His physical
lt, he has brought you into his own presence, and you are holy and blameless as you
im without a single fault. 23 But you must continue to believe this truth and sta
Don't drift away from the assurance you received when you heard the Good News. Th
as been preached all over the world, and I, Paul, have been appointed as God's serv
im it. 24 I am glad when I suffer for you in my body, for I am participating in the su
ist that continue for His body, the church. 25 God has given me the responsibility of
urch by proclaiming His entire message to you. 26 This message was kept secret for
nerations past, but now it has been revealed to God's people. 27 For God wanted them
e riches and glory of Christ are for you Gentiles, too. And this is the secret: Chris
This gives you assurance of sharing His glory. 28 So we tell others about Christ,

Contents

Introduction

I REMEMBER LIKE YESTERDAY what it felt like to be fresh off the plane from a completely different culture and enter a world I knew nothing about. My ninth-grade year was a confusing blur of living in America after spending most of my childhood as a missionary kid in Thailand. I attended a local high school in Massachusetts, and I clearly remember the school building, which resembled a jail and had a creepy basement full of pipes that hung low from the ceiling. I was constantly anxious, and underneath everything was the feeling that I did not belong in America, but I didn't fully belong in Thailand either. I was your typical third-culture kid—like a key that kept getting jammed into the wrong door. Unable to fit, I could not quite unlock my own identity.

How would my life have looked different if I had never come to America from Thailand? I often wonder who I would be if I had stayed all my life in the same house and never moved continents or homes. Suppose I had never lived in the bamboo huts or smack-dab in the middle of the city. Pretend I had never taken all those cross-continental trips. How would my perspective be different? I could read about lands I had not been to and know in part what I was missing out on. But it's a completely different concept to actually go somewhere—to taste and see. There is nothing like experiencing the strawberries plucked directly from the bush or feeling the brisk and windy New England fall with its myriad of colorful trees and crunchy fallen leaves. Cultures shape our perspective, and with each new experience, we grow in what we know.

I have used a variety of transportation methods in my lifetime. I was brought to school by a rickshaw—a man pedaling a bicycle with us kids sitting in the back of the cushioned open-air vehicle.

With each new experience, we grow in what we know.

I have been escorted around town on a motorbike and a dirt bike, and I've had my fill of tuk-tuks (three-wheeled motorbike contraptions) and songthaews (bus-like public transport vehicles). The airplane revolutionized transportation, and I have been on airplanes countless times. Every time I bring one of my babies on the airplane, the flight attendant asks, "Is this his first flight?"

"Nope, he has traveled quite a bit," I banter back.

Airplanes have changed what we can see, experience, and learn. Like an airplane, the Inductive Bible Study method can transport you to a new vantage point. It can take you to a land that I truly hope you will make your life in: the Bible. It's a land that, if you choose to live in it, will produce fruit by the power of the Holy Spirit dwelling in you. A land where you will learn and lean into God. A land where you will realize that God is ever present. A land where your heart can be trained to see His daily provision for your every need. May the Inductive Bible Study method awaken you to God's wisdom, depth, and love. May you till the soil, excavate the text, and find that amid all your exploring, you long for Christ—and for His will to be done in your life.

In a far greater way than modern transportation, the Bible has profoundly impacted humanity. The Bible is the most influential book in the world. Its writing took place over a span of 1,500 to

1,600 years on three different continents. The Bible has stood the test of time, and we see this over and over again. I remember reading about a Bible that was found intact after the 9/11 World Trade Center terrorist attack. According to an article in *Christianity Today*, "Somewhere inside the National September 11 Memorial & Museum in New York City is a big chunk of metal fused to a Bible. Well, half a Bible. Its scorched pages are open to Matthew 5, the Sermon on the Mount. An anonymous firefighter reportedly found the artifact in the rubble under the South Tower of the World Trade Center. Now it's on display as what a 9/11 photographer called a reminder 'that the Bible's message survives throughout time.'"[1] That feels like a metaphor to me about how nothing can obstruct God's Word. It doesn't fade, it doesn't become outdated, it can't be smothered by natural phenomena or human interference.

It is in this remarkable book that we draw near to God, and He draws near to us. As Psalm 34:8 says, "Taste and see that the LORD is good; blessed is the one who takes refuge in him." Dwell upon His words as you taste His goodness. As we take refuge in the pages of Scripture, we find a *who* at the end of the journey: a God who loves us and desires to have a relationship with us. A God bent on His pursuit of us. He is within us and around us, and He communicates to us through the pages of Scripture. What great news that He has made His dwelling in our hearts!

If I had never come to America, I would have fared differently in small ways. But if I had never known the Bible, I would be different in ways that I can't comprehend.

If I Had Never Read the Word of God

If I had never read the Bible, I would have never dared pray the prayers I've prayed through the Word of God. My fear never would have dissipated. My heart never would have calmed at the words in this book. The Bible has taught me of God's mercy, which I never would have plumbed without His Word. It is through the pages of Scripture I have tasted His extravagant love, His willingness to chase me down. Through the Bible, my heart has been tuned to know God, and through the pages of Scripture I hear a melody of His character:

If I had never known the Bible, I would be different in ways that I can't comprehend.

> The LORD, the LORD, the compassionate and gracious God, slow to anger, abounding in love and faithfulness, maintaining love to thousands, and forgiving wickedness, rebellion and sin. Yet he does not leave the guilty unpunished; he punishes the children and their children for the sin of the parents to the third and fourth generation.
>
> EXODUS 34:6-7

As my son reminded me recently, flamingos are pink because they eat shrimp, and carrots can turn you orange. What we feast our hearts on will eventually come out of our mouths and work its way into our conduct. When we behold God's law and read His Word, our lives are forever changed and we grow in the fruit of the Spirit.

If I Had Never Found Inductive Bible Study

If I had never boarded the airplane all those times to make the long trek across the ocean to America, I would never have fully comprehended this culture. In a similar way, if I had never found Inductive Bible Study, I know God would have been gracious to reveal to me much about His Word, but I don't believe I would understand the Bible at the depth I do now.

While I was getting my MA in practical theology, God used Inductive Bible Study to transform my life. As I sat in on my first hermeneutics class as a mom of two kids, the professor explained we would need to root ourselves in the historical context and find at least ten to fifteen observations in the text. I remember being overwhelmed at the thought *How will I find that many observations in this passage?*

But in that class, I was trained to *see* what was already there.

We live in a sound-bite culture, barely able to focus on one thing for long. Our attention spans have dropped to around 8.25 seconds, shorter than that of a goldfish.[2] When it comes to spiritual matters, this does not bode well for us because studying God's Word takes time.

In our jam-packed lives, it is becoming increasingly difficult to convince people that there is value in spending time saturating oneself in the Word. Some people manage to complete Bible-in-a-year plans, and there's no doubt a benefit of getting a rooftop view of the whole Scriptures. Reading the Bible in a year is a wonderful, time-consuming goal. But slowly studying a passage of Scripture and seeking to understand its context is a completely different matter. Many times I've felt like I knew a country after going on a short-term mission trip or running around as a tourist. Yet it was not until I lived in America that I truly understood what the culture is like. Similarly, we can feel like we know the Bible through just a surface reading of the text. It takes work to slow down and spend adequate time in God's Word, and it is rare to find others doing the same. On this path, you read God's Word with no other intention but to really know Him. On this path, you spend enough time with God to gain His perspective, testing the familiar sayings that are meant to encourage us but in reality are often taken out of context.

Although it's not easy to chart your own course, may I ask you to consider doing it with me?

If there is anyone who felt like they had a monopoly on Scripture it was me, a child of Bible translators who brought me up in the faith. I was raised on every Bible story, and I learned to recite verses when I was a young child. As an adult, the biggest obstacle to my desire to go deeper was actually my assumption that I already knew a lot about the Bible—that I already knew how to study it. But as I quickly found out, I still had much to learn.

I originally went back to school to get my master's because I had just started my ministry, Chasing Sacred. Through this ministry, I shared about God's Word and how it applied to my life. Soon I realized people were listening, and it would be best if I knew what I was talking about. That's what sent me back to school, and Chasing Sacred grew dramatically through its sales of our Inductive Bible Study journal. In the journal, I teach people how to study the Bible by asking them a series of questions in a journal format. My church so graciously adopted this method, and we used the journal to go through different books of the Bible in our women's Bible study.

My mind flashes back to a memory in my church lobby. I turned to get my coffee and smiled at the woman next to me. She beckoned me closer. "Thirty-eight! Thirty-eight," she said again. "I was thirty-eight when I learned how to study the Bible." I listened intently as she continued. "I was thirty-eight when I did your journal on Inductive Bible Study, and for the first time, I understood why we study the Bible in its original context, why we ask questions of the text. I finally understood why it is important to study it systematically. This is the first time in my life that I am getting something out of the Word! That's what I told a friend recently, at least. She said she opens up the Word and doesn't even know where to begin! I told her to do the method you teach in your journal."

I couldn't have smiled bigger. This woman had been transported via aircraft to a new land, and she was gaining a deeper understanding of the Word of God for the first time!

Although we're often preoccupied with our age, don't let that be a hang-up or frustration when you read this book. God speaks no matter how young or old you are! No opposition can come between Him and His children.

Can the Inductive Bible Study method help you? Yes! Is this method inspired? No! But can it guide you in your study and make the Word come alive to you? Yes!

There is no one right way to study the Bible. There is no perfect time of day, either—Bible reading looks different in every season. What I do know is that the Bible will change your life, just like learning to study it in-depth changed mine. It will change your outlook on so many things.

Reading God's Word in an orderly way is like cleaning and tidying your house. If my home is cluttered, it is a lot harder to vacuum and mop without bumping into things. But once I've cleaned and ordered my house, I can see more clearly what else needs work. In the same way, an orderly method to approaching God's Word in your personal Bible study will lead to much fruit. My personal hope is that when you close this book, you will be so excited about studying God's Word in this way that you won't be able to stop yourself from sharing it with others. My hope is that the joy of studying the Bible in its cultural and historical context will bring clarity, excitement, and engagement for you in your Scripture reading. My hope is that you will look forward to opening the pages of Scripture every single day, excitedly anticipating hearing from God, and that you will grow in your love of Him through these pages.

PART I

Why Chase Sacred?

FIND SOMETHING WORTH
CHASING AFTER

I GLANCED OVER AT MY MOM, and she looked tired. Our family had been hit with wave after wave of misfortune, and it was beginning to take a toll. This was the second time our house in Thailand had flooded during my tenth-grade year—the same year my parents were turning in their translation of the New Testament. It could have been coincidental, but we had never experienced so many things going wrong at once. The entire downstairs of our home was engulfed in water. We sandbagged the doors, but that did not stop the water from rushing in. We watched the water come for us, our furniture, my sister's room, and our dining room. The cockroaches knew the water was coming, and it was no longer safe for them in the drains. They scurried excitedly out to greet us. I got the broom and valiantly fought the good fight while my siblings screamed on the bench. Me against the millions of cockroaches.

We sandbagged and bailed water into the night. Our good friend, the lead national translator, helped us scoop buckets of water out the windows, but the attempts seemed futile. No matter how long we bailed, the water kept surging in. I could tell my mom and dad felt terrible. They felt bad about the last year of chaos in America we had experienced. They felt bad that now we were back in Thailand, we all had recently been sick with dengue fever, my sister was going through an additional health battle, and our house was probably going to grow black mold. They felt bad that tomorrow was my brother's birthday, and most likely we would have to spend it huddled in our upstairs as we watched our downstairs drown.

We woke up the following day to our neighbors making pancakes, and we enjoyed pancakes and laughter as we looked at the mess of our first floor. After breakfast, we waded out of our house, waist-deep in water, and caught a ride in a boat. This was the first—and, I am sure, last—time I would ride a boat down a usually busy road full of traffic that had succumbed to being a river.

Then and Now

The back-and-forth season of my family's misfortune had one stable anchor: the Bible. I began each day with a "Dear God" entry in my journal with my Bible open beside me. I look back at the childish script and picture what was happening in my mind then. I had no clue about the deeper truths within the Bible. But isn't that what is so beautiful about grace? We never genuinely know where we were until after we have left. I am convinced that sometimes God's grace can close our eyes to our ignorance or missteps at the time, and it is not until we turn back that we see how far we have come. The clarity of hindsight often reminds me that Christ instigates heart change and works everything out in His timing.

I know God was in my Bible study then, just as He's in my Bible study now! He was in it when it was me-centric, and He is in it now that I want to go deeper. My approach to Bible study when I was young was not wrong, but I am so thankful now that I know what I know. At that time, I thought I was chasing God, but as I've grown older and wiser, I have realized that He has always been in relentless pursuit of me.

As I studied back then, I felt the Holy Spirit working in my life and mind. Now when I study, I feel the same thing—but I have more clarity, and I've grown in my understanding of the Bible. How does each book fit into the whole? Why does historical context matter? What in the world does the Old Testament have to do with the New Testament? I am so excited to explore these questions with you as we grow together in this book.

During my younger years, I was weighed down by not understanding what was happening to my family. Why was life so hard at that time? Looking back now, I can see that my parents pointed me toward God's Word no matter what chaos was unfolding in our lives. A deep respect for and dependence on God's Word permeated our home. Every morning when I woke up, I saw my parents, coffee in hand, poring over the Scriptures. I remember nights of fellowship around the dinner table as I got older, participating in Scripture memory as a family. My mom perched a small notebook of verses on our car's dashboard, and the lined notebook would go on outdoor runs with her as she committed them to memory. I mean, we nicknamed my mom Holy Mother because of her affinity for the Word of God.

Flash forward. As an adult, before I learned the Inductive Bible

> *At that time, I thought I was chasing God, but as I've grown older and wiser, I have realized that He has always been in relentless pursuit of me.*

Study method, I often sat with my Bible open, trying to make sense of the familiar Scripture verses at hand. I realized they were *too* familiar. I wanted a new word from God—something exciting and different. As a seasoned believer, I had heard the gospel so many times, and I believed that I knew everything there was to know about the Word of God. I longed for a new outlook—and this is often where the devil plants his seed of confusion, *in familiarity.* Those of us who grew up in the church all our lives might think we know too much. Others of us may feel we don't know enough. Maybe you are beginning this Inductive Bible Study journey in your sixties, and you have studied the Word your entire life. Or maybe you are a new believer trying to read and understand the Bible, but digging in seems daunting and scary.

I knew the time I spent in the Bible was essential for life, and I hungered for it. I knew every Bible story inside and out, but I lacked the tools to go deeper and really study God's Word. When we become that familiar with the Word of God, we can think we know it too well to be a beginner again. We might say to ourselves, *I've read these stories a thousand times. What more am I supposed to get out of reading God's Word? Now, what was that influencer saying on Instagram yesterday?* Assuming that God's Word is static and boring is the biggest obstacle to curiosity and learning. Being a new believer actually puts you ahead of the game in Bible study, providing fresh ground and fresh soil for these new truths—without old weeds that need to be dug up and old perspectives that need uprooting. It's a fresh start!

I remember, as a teen, clinging to the pages of the Bible for comfort through a season of depression. The Bible then became a lifeline of hope during difficult college years and cross-cultural moves. I have one specific memory of going to New Hampshire to stay with my grandparents on college break. My parents were still in Thailand, so I could only go home for Christmas. I was navigating a complicated friendship at the time, and I was exhausted by how this friendship was unfolding. With my parents so far away, it was hard to confide in them. I had to catch them early in the morning or late at night because of the time difference.

But my grandparents had the warmest, coziest, most rug-laden house. It was so quiet there I could barely sleep. Every morning, I cracked open my Bible and gathered my journal, which I wrote in daily. I stumbled down the stairs and smelled the New England Coffee hazelnut-flavored brew. Small sticky notes accompanied the two pots of brewed coffee. In bold type, one read DECAF and the other read REGULAR. I would pour myself a coffee and then bring down a few of the cups I had hoarded that week to stash in the dishwasher before anyone noticed. As I opened the dishwasher, I noticed another sticky note that read DIRTY. I laughed as I imagined my grandfather scrawling on colorful sticky pads to ensure I knew what was happening in the house. My favorite note showed up after I found his stash of chocolate. He must have noticed because, after that, the chocolate was labeled with a new sticky note: CHOCOLATE FOR BRIDGE. He played bridge with a few friends, and I must have gotten into their available reserve.

I often searched the Bible for directions like these sticky notes. In every memory, I can point to many sticky-note moments that directed my path: a verse that comforted me, convicted me, or showed me which step to take next. Sometimes I felt like my mind was going a million miles a minute, and I would stop and open my Bible, only to find what felt like a sticky note addressed to me. I viewed the Bible as a book whose main purpose was to provide specific direction for my life. I had placed myself center stage as the main character in the Bible stories I read, and the "villain" was whatever problem or frustration I was facing in my life at the time. I navigated the Bible like a self-help book, seeking out any kind of assurance for my heart within its pages. My thinking was simple:

The Scriptures were written so I could distill meaning out of my life, right? In my mind, the Bible became a list of pragmatic ideas that helped its readers become better people, and along the way, it provided much-needed answers to *my* problems. The possibility that the Bible could lead to so much more, to a life of awe and reverence and intimacy with God—well, somehow, I had missed that part.

And no one challenged my eager but inadequate fumbling through the text. It was like I was taking in a mountain of information without having someone explain, *really explain* the principles of Bible study. Though I daily delighted in God's Word, no one helped me understand that this experience could go beyond my personal interpretations and emotional reactions. I hadn't entertained the idea that, beyond the way I felt or applied this book to my life, there was a world within its pages waiting to engage my brain and help me genuinely comprehend God's message and character. That deeper understanding would make all the difference in how I lived my life in God's ordered world.

I navigated the Bible like a self-help book, seeking out any kind of assurance for my heart within its pages.

Countless themes and principles work their way through the Bible, which is made up of sixty-six books in various literary genres written by numerous authors across many historical periods. Still, the Bible speaks one consistent message: the story of God's love and His redemption of humankind.

Beginning Again

I have approached Bible study in a myriad of ways in my lifetime. I have cherry-picked passages that seemed relevant to me and have lost sight of the context. I have missed how a particular passage fits into the overarching narrative of the Bible. It was not until attending Bible college as an adult to pursue a master's in practical theology that I truly changed my approach to studying the Scriptures. But I do not feel any of those years of searching the text and reading in a me-centric way was a waste. I believe God uses every season of our Bible study journey. When I took my first class in hermeneutics—"the science and art of biblical interpretation"—it was an *aha* moment.[1] Suddenly, as I began to read the text afresh, I realized I could *observe* the text before applying it. I could ask questions about the Scripture passage, and I could go beyond just using the text to explain myself and understand what it meant as a whole. It was as if I were beginning again. The Bible took on new breadth and meaning in my life.

As Martin Luther stated, "To progress is always to begin again."[2] So there I sat, now an adult in my first hermeneutics class, and I had the breath knocked out of me. In this class, we looked at what a text meant to the original audience. Once we had a good grasp of the context, we could exegete (interpret) it. The tools of hermeneutics allowed us to bridge the cultural and historical gap to determine how the passage applies in our own culture and times. We dove deep and slow into one specific passage. I loved how this style of learning opened up my knowledge of the Bible in a way I had never anticipated.

I remember opening my computer during my kids' nap time and the professor beginning to instruct us on proper exegesis. Exegesis means the interpretation of a Scripture text. In this particular instance, I did not realize how much critical thinking could go into studying a passage of Scripture. There were methods and instructions that I hadn't even known existed. Nap time was my opportunity to enter my Narnia, this new world of Bible study I was so unfamiliar with but wanted to learn about. We were going through the book of Mark, and all of a sudden, the questions our professor was teaching us to ask of the text made the passages come to light like they never had before. He also structured the process in a way that I could understand. He brought us through the three steps of Inductive Bible Study, which I will talk more about later in this book: observation, interpretation, and application.

I could not believe all the information I could glean from the passage once I was equipped to ask the right questions. It was like reading the ingredients list on the back of a box and understanding it for the first time. As a child, I used to look at ingredient lists in ignorant bliss. Now, as an adult, when I read one of these lists, I know that propylene glycol—a common addition to our food—is also used in antifreeze, and L-cysteine, which is a protein from human hair, is keeping our bread fresh on the shelves. In the same way, the Inductive Bible Study method awakened a whole new world for me! Suddenly I was informed—but in the best way possible, not the worst way possible. I started to see treasures, not horrific ingredients.

Thus I began a new adventure in discovering that there was and is *so much* to learn about the Bible. No matter how long you've been a believer, if you have not had the opportunity to understand how to really study God's Word, I want to encourage you that a whole world of relationship and intimacy and knowledge of God awaits you. I recently needed to pick a class for my master's in theology, and I saw a course titled Social Media in Ministry. I scoffed a little, thinking I could teach that class with my eyes closed. *I have a thriving online ministry. I teach on social media every day. I don't see the need to teach this seasoned Instagrammer anything.* But the truth is that *progress often requires us to begin again.* In the end, I did learn much from the class that I thought I had mastered.

Often we want new knowledge, and many times this desire for something new—some new vision that's more current and exciting—eclipses the need to maintain our allegiance to the truth of the gospel. The truth of Christ must always remain preeminent. And so, I realized my longing was for growth, and when we look deeper into Martin Luther's words about beginning again, we understand that growth is simple. It is learning to begin again. It is learning to take a fresh look at the Word of God and sit with the truths of the gospel again. God reveals Himself to us through the world that He created and through Scripture (sometimes called general revelation and special revelation respectively). Nature shows us so much about who our Creator God is, and Scripture is His Word breathed out to humanity. We need to interpret Scripture in light of what other scholars and commentaries have confirmed. We will never receive unique disclosures that do not align with God's closed special revelation: the Bible. What that means is that our baseline for any divine knowledge or truth is the Word of God. If it doesn't line up with Scripture, I do not want it!

Growth and learning happen when we choose to abide in the Lord through reading His Word. Intimacy with God starts here. We can begin again every morning when we open the pages of our Bible and prepare to learn more about our heavenly Father. We read the Word of God to get to know who He is, and in turn we understand more about who we are as well. Then we practice how to live through experiences in Christ-centered community, and we practice how to love like Christ through fellowship with a body of believers. But we must not let ourselves speak for Scripture, interpreting only in the light of our personal experience. Instead, we can let Scripture speak for itself and interpret our experiences in context of what it says.

Chasing What's Important

It is in the process of starting over that we realize: We need humility when we open the Bible. We need to be curious and have a beginner's heart. If we don't get rid of our pretenses, we will not be able to slow down and observe anew. It is time to throw out our old, bad habits of picking a random verse or passage and letting it tell us truths about ourselves only. Instead, let's learn to take the big picture of God's Word into account. In doing so, we will encounter Christ and His death and resurrection, and we'll learn about God's character.

My six-year-old son is learning how to read. It has been my delight and joy to watch him go from a world of ignorant bliss to a world of informed curiosity! He is a very slow reader. But he spends every waking minute now trying to piece together words to learn how to read. He does not read fluently, and he frequently makes mistakes. Yet he lets himself be a beginner, and I teach him that the more curious he is, the more he will learn. He does not rush ahead to the next word but instead slowly sounds out each letter of the word he's on. In this book, I hope to teach you a slower method of ingesting Scripture, a method *for really observing the text*. My goal is to see you move from a new or novice reader of the Scriptures to a literate student of His Word. It will take patience, but it is such a delight as a believer to go from infancy in the knowledge of God to mature delight in His Word. What if we let ourselves be beginners again with the Word of God? Just as my son works diligently to become a fluent reader, can we move forward diligently to study and learn God's Word?

The inductive method is a slowed-down approach to Bible study. It is the opposite of a reading plan where we rush to get to the finish line. It is a way of studying where we carefully read each word and consider why it is there. It is taking small chunks of Scripture in context and asking questions of the text to get at its original intent. It takes you through a three-step process of question asking, starting with observing the text, then interpreting it, and finally applying it. Often we jump ahead to the application, which is not necessarily wrong, but we miss so much of the depth of Bible study when we only understand how it applies to us. When we use the Inductive Bible Study method, we are first and foremost seeking to know how the Bible verse fits into the grand story of Scripture, what it tells us about God's character, and what the letter, prophecy, or historical account meant to its original audience. I love the inductive method of Bible study because we don't skip around in Scripture but read it *all*, even the parts that don't appear to apply to us at the moment. We choose to meditate on beautiful truths that might have been skipped over if we had a bad morning and only wanted to settle on a section of text that moved the needle on our "self-development." Inductive Bible Study encourages us to sit, observe, meditate, and apply what God is teaching us. The inductive method does this primarily through its *W* and *H* questions: Who, What, Where, When, Why, and How help us to discern the meaning of the text. We will go deeper into these practical logistics of Inductive Bible Study later in this book.

In our increasingly chaotic world, it is such a comfort to have the Bible, which is steady, unwavering, and thoroughly reliable. While media seeks to focus our eyes on the here and now and all there is to fear, Scripture will always speak truth to our souls. It stands as a steady barometer of right, wrong, and everything in between. What a joy!

Peter testifies to the trustworthiness of the Scriptures. He wants us to understand what a privilege we have as believers: "We have even greater confidence in the message proclaimed by the prophets. You must pay close attention to what they wrote, for their words are like a lamp shining in a dark place—until the Day dawns, and Christ the Morning Star shines in your hearts" (2 Peter 1:19, NLT). We will do well to pay attention to God's Word. It is a light that illuminates our way. God's first words in Genesis were "Let there be light" (Genesis 1:3), and Scripture continues to illuminate our lives, clear up confusion, and bring us into intimate fellowship with our Father. The light of Scripture sweeps away the chaos of unexpected news, tumultuous relationships, and feelings of fear and doubt.

With all the things vying for our attention these days, are we giving God's Word its rightful place in our lives? Are we chasing what's important? It is easy to run headfirst in a myriad of directions, whether it is finding comfort, looking for importance in education and accolades, or doing what feels right in the moment. I have spent decades chasing many different things, but none of these pursuits have been as life-changing as chasing God. I have a specific memory of when the Lord prompted me to slow down in chasing influence, persuasion, and meaning and instead chase the One from whom all these things naturally flow. I was holding my son, who was a baby at the time, and he grabbed the water I had just set on the table. It spilled all over him. I just remember thinking that we often grab that which we cannot hold. A lofty and meaningful chase, however, will always lead to God. Every day we are bombarded with the message that certain products will make our lives better. Yet we have over one hundred different translations of the English Bible at our fingertips—are we availing ourselves of this priceless resource? Don't let the excitement of Scripture be lost on you. Before we continue our journey into this book, please pray this prayer with me: *Lord, give me the desire to understand Your Word, and help me grow closer to You through this book.*

EXPERIENCE THE DELIGHT
OF GOD'S WORD

MY NOW-HUSBAND AND I BROKE UP in college after a year and a half of dating, and I was ready to run in the opposite direction as fast as possible. I turned my face to the sun, and I was moving on to better prospects. My husband was not. He was not done chasing after me. He wanted me back. He was in New Hampshire, and I was doing school in Michigan, so he was not physically present, yet it felt like he followed me everywhere I went.

I walked to my local college coffee shop one day, and the barista proclaimed, "You have a gift card here from Jamie?"

"Yes," I muttered. "Hmmm . . ." I accepted it but felt annoyed.

Easter came, and an Easter basket with my name *engraved* on it arrived at my college mail center. I could not believe my eyes. "Whaaaat?" I tossed it aside. My dance recital came, and so did a big bouquet and chocolate-covered strawberries that my roommates devoured. I could not shake this guy, I tell ya! It was not until a burned CD of love songs showed up—featuring a picture of us on its cover and a song with the chorus "I'll take you back"—that I called him. "Pleeease stop pursuing me! I am not interested!" He did finally win me back by sending me on a surprise scavenger hunt around New York City. We are happily married now!

In an even greater way, God pursues us, and one of the ways He demonstrates His love for us is through His Word. He chases us down and speaks to us through His living, breathing Word. Scripture tells us that God draws us into a loving relationship with Him: "No one can come to me unless the Father who sent me draws him. And I will raise him up on the last day" (John 6:44, ESV). The entirety of the Bible is about God's chase of humankind, His desire for relationship with us, and how He woos us to Himself. Even in our stubbornness and our doubts, He is relentless in coming after us.

At first I thought I had found God through His Word, but I now know He has found me! The parable of the lost sheep (see Luke 15:1-7) illustrates how God searches for us, finds us, and brings us into a loving relationship with Him. God calls us by name and is intimately acquainted with our comings and goings (see Psalm 139:1-3). So how can we respond to God's pursuit of us? We can chase Him right back.

The entirety of the Bible is about God's chase of humankind, His desire for relationship with us, and how He woos us to Himself.

I love what Psalm 14:2 says: "The LORD looks down from heaven on the entire human race; he looks to see if anyone is truly wise, if anyone seeks God" (NLT).

Chasing Sacred

As I corral my five kids into the car for the trip to women's Bible study, buckle the millions of car seats, and cram my notebook and Bible into my overstuffed diaper bag, I feel like a wild horse. Too stubborn to call it quits. My oldest two had school canceled last minute, leaving me, the study leader, with an SUV of chaos. As I grip my Bible tightly, I realize that I often feel like leading this study is the last thing I should be doing. Sometimes I'm not sure if what I am doing really matters. Not sure I should be teaching the Bible to a group of women when I have five kids in tow. I linger a little longer with this thought before I park my vehicle at the church. I glance quickly at my watch. I look over my Inductive Bible Study notes. This is something I have spent so many hours teaching, I have committed it to memory. I remind myself that, like a dancer who moves effortlessly through her rehearsed moves, I could proclaim every part of the inductive method without skipping a beat. I take a quick swig of my coffee as I try to jam the lidless cup into the center console without spilling it. Where is that to-go cup I just bought? Thirsty for water, and trying to figure out how I am going to transport my box of journals, bulging diaper bag, and all the kids to the front door of the church, I try to dismiss my worries. *I'm here, aren't I?*

What should life be like for a frazzled, trying-to-be-faithful mom of five? Is there one way to do this thing right? As I open the trunk, the journals I created to teach women about the Inductive Bible Study method come tumbling out, and I barely catch them with my foot as I pinch my chin tighter around my pen. Even in the midst of the chaos, I realize there's nothing I'd rather be doing with my time. I love this.

I did not step gingerly into my Inductive Bible Study obsession.

Like most things in life that I like to do, I took the plunge with more gusto than knowledge, passion than expertise, and energy than craft. From the very start, I was enthusiastic, excited, energetic, and eager to tell everyone about this life-changing method.

Going Too Fast

You might find stories like this humorous, but my bosses did not. I had three jobs in college: I worked at a theater, as a student driver, and as a waitress at the Wooden Shoe Restaurant. The Wooden Shoe was a breakfast place known for its *huge* cinnamon rolls and twelve-egg omelet challenge—if you could finish the whole omelet, you got a T-shirt. (I never tried.) The loyal customers tended to be mainly from the oatmeal generation.

Tuesdays ran at a different rhythm and my manager definitely did not enjoy them. On Tuesdays, residents from a nearby nursing home would roll in on a big bus. They sipped their coffee, asked for extra brown sugar, and rewarded service with gumball-machine-sized tips. I just thought perhaps they hadn't kept up with best practices on tipping and didn't know any better. One day as I closed up, I was asked to prefill the next day's little brown sugar cups. Motivated, and figuring I could work twice as fast and do more than necessary, I set to work filling those cups. In my mind, I would be making my tattooed, Harley-Davidson-riding manager proud. So I filled up *twice* as many brown sugars as she asked for.

The next day, my manager stormed into the restaurant. "Whooo filled up all those extra brown sugar containers?" She glanced at me.

"I did," I confessed, wondering why she was upset at my willingness to go the extra mile.

"If you prefill too many brown sugars, they go bad. They'll get all dry and stale, and it's a waste. Don't do that again."

Apparently working ahead to save yourself the trouble the next day doesn't always pan out, even when you have good intentions. In this case, my efforts mirrored the biblical story of the Israelites trying to save manna for the next day's meal when God had clearly said He would provide their food daily. When the Israelites tried to save extra, they ended up with rotten manna the next day (see Exodus 16:1-31).

It sure seems like a good principle: if you work ahead, you can take the day off tomorrow. In some situations, this is a very wise thing to do. But I have also learned that some rhythms with God don't align with that mentality. Just like manna, God gave us His Word to be savored daily, and any attempt to store up God's Word on Sunday so that we can slide our way through the rest of the week without effort is a lesson in futility. We end up lacking the very nutrients, the nourishment we need daily to walk according to God's plan for us. Jesus taught us to pray, "Give us this day our daily bread" (Matthew 6:11, ESV), suggesting He took it for granted we would spend time with God every day. And unlike with chocolate cake, we cannot ever overindulge on God's Word. No time in Scripture is ever wasted. There are some days when all we get is a small portion, and God graciously uses one small verse to powerfully speak to our hearts. And there are some days when we receive bountifully.

Let's be honest. The everyday craziness of life—the continuous needs of family, frustrations in our relationships, bills we hadn't planned for—distracts our hearts and minds from hearing God's voice. And there are so many things in this world that we enjoy chasing after. While they bring temporary distraction and even fun, they cannot compete with relating to God our Father. When I choose to daily set my face toward learning more about Him, I am never disappointed. God graciously left us a road

No time in Scripture is ever wasted.

map to life, the most important book in all the world, the book that enables us to navigate every twist and turn. The Bible is rarely far from us physically, but it's often far from our hearts. We often choose to do anything but spend time in God's Word. But let's face it—we're never going to stop hearing the incessant call of the world telling us that we will and should find meaning and satisfaction in our families, our health, or perhaps our dream jobs. Yet as we live through our next challenge, climb that corporate ladder, or observe the havoc that sinful humanity can unleash, again and again we find ourselves wondering about that void in our hearts that can only be filled by our Creator. *Is this it?* we wonder. Our spirits feel restless, unsatisfied until we access the treasure that God has already given us, the Bible. The Bible points us to the ultimate treasure, the ultimate prize: Christ Himself.

God promises His Word will never return void (see Isaiah 55:11). It will surely have an impact on us and on others. That's a promise from God. It is only in His Word that we will find truth that remains through all generations and can personally give us hope. When we set aside time to read and meditate on the Scriptures, God will transform us as we learn more about Him! Over time, we will learn how to love both God and others on a deeper level. God's mercies do exist, and they are waiting to be discovered in His Word.

My job as a student driver was just plain easy and fun. All I had to do was transport students who did not have their own cars to places they needed to go off campus. Which meant I got paid to sit and do my homework until someone called and needed to go somewhere. Not only was this the best job ever, but I also had a wonderful boss. Her name was Shelly, and she had fiery-red hair. We clicked immediately, and she adopted me on day one. It was her job to tell me who I needed to drive and where I should take them.

One day, Shelly called me aside. She looked sheepish and hesitant. "Mikella, you took a speed bump too fast. That girl who was riding with you, you made her nervous. Can you perhaps slow down a bit? Especially on account that it *is* snowing today." This was the first time I had seen the serious Shelly. And I know it pained her to have to confront me.

I wasn't upset with Shelly, but I confess that I was very upset with that girl who thought I was driving too fast. Didn't she enjoy getting some air on the speed bumps? Slowing down went against the fiber of my being. I was my grandmother's child, and my grandmother only knew one speed: fast. When she pulled into her driveway, she was out of the car before it even had the chance to stop!

Truth be told, I went everywhere fast, always chasing something. I had already spent a great deal of my life chasing dance, which was my love and a serious discipline for me. I had also chased love, meaning, and other things I thought would fulfill me. I think that's a pretty common tendency. What's not as common is turning our attention to a spiritual chasing of God. And that was where I needed to slow down and focus.

The Turning Point

It was during this formative period in college, as I waitressed or drove students to their destinations, that I started chasing something different. The change came when I mysteriously got a condition called drop foot and I could not dance for a full semester. Without realizing it, I began chasing what was eternal. I began chasing sacred. I attended weekly Bible studies, volunteered to help troubled youth, attended a local church, and began reading my Bible for two hours every morning. I woke up each day at 5 a.m. to really study God's Word.

My faith was growing, and I was taking ownership of it. I could have made so many other choices during those precious college years, but I think my faith was incentivized by the limo that brought me to church every week. A guy who owned a limo service volunteered to pick up my friends and me each week since we didn't have our own vehicles. If God is calling the youth, you might as well pick them up in a limo!

The first time I remember doing deep, deep Bible study beyond just applying Scripture to myself was in one of these college Bible studies. Every other Friday, one of the dance professors and her friends would spend all day cooking, and they would pick up my dance friends and me to feed us and spend hours and hours in the Word with us. Those girls and I would read sections of Scripture out loud and discuss it, and the time would fly. I loved every second of it. I couldn't stop—I just kept chasing after God through His Word. Like a lawn sprinkler, when I was connected to the spigot of His Word, the ground around me remained fertile.

Not everyone was enthused with what I was gaining. I remember calling home on one instance with questions. I had attended a Bible study in my dorm, and I'd shared with some of the other group members how God had spoken to my heart. One of the leaders, a kind, elderly Reformed brother, responded, "I don't think so. . . . He did not speak to you that way. He only speaks through His Word."

At the time, I was upset. How could this man tell me that God was not the source of my prompting, that what I believed God was speaking to me was in fact not from God at all? Confused, I wondered, *Do I not know His voice?* So I did what a bewildered daughter of Christian upbringing does when faced with uncertainty in her spiritual walk—I asked my mom and dad. I was used to speaking with them about every frustration and faith-based question. They would patiently seek to provide explanations and input on whatever questions I brought them. They explained to me that depending on your denomination, the way you understood God's revelation could vary. This was a great reminder to me that God may speak to our hearts, but His voice will always align with Scripture. That's why it's so important for us to know Scripture: so we're familiar with His voice and can make sure a message is from Him.

If you think I chased after God purely because I was interested in spiritual things, that's not the full picture. Looking back, I know what also kept my nose in the Word all those years: depression. It had started after my bout with dengue fever in Thailand. Dengue fever and depression are often linked, but I did not know that at the time. I was only fifteen when my struggle with depression began, and it would rear its ugly head repeatedly through the years. And in college, my depression was at its all-time worst. I was drowning and I needed God desperately, so I found myself intent on reading and studying His Word.

Delight and Duty

Let's take a few minutes to talk about delight and duty. If we're honest, there's a certain amount of both duty and delight mixed into the Christian life. When we wake up early in the morning to spend time reading God's Word, it may initially feel like duty—and it may be the last thing we want to do. Maybe we're exhausted from staying up late the night before. Maybe we are harboring sin and don't want to be convicted by our Bible. Or maybe we are so discouraged with life that we think reading Scripture would be in vain. I urge you to remember that we have an enemy who is furiously intent on distracting us from all that God has for us. Don't let him do it. On the other side of choosing to open God's Word—even when we don't feel like it—we often discover a fountain of delight.

The idea of delight occurs approximately 110 times in Scripture in various forms. Less than fifteen occurrences are found in the New Testament. . . . [In the Old Testament,] two of the most common Hebrew terms for delight are *hepes*, "to bend towards, to be inclined towards [an object or person]," and *rasa*, "to delight or take pleasure in."[1]

In the Bible, *delight* often relates to God's Word or God's law. How can we express to God that we are really listening? We open our Bibles (or Bible apps) and really lean into the words on those pages, we take notes, and we let God's Word saturate our whole being. This is real listening to our Father—and how could God not be pleased when we take His Word seriously and delight in His law? The psalmist describes the righteous person this way: "His delight is in the law of the LORD, and on his law he meditates day and night" (Psalm 1:2, ESV).

As we truly listen to God speak through Scripture, we delight in God Himself. It is within the pages of the Bible that we get to know our God, and the more we know Him, the more we love Him. When I think about this, I imagine my mom and dad exegeting the meaning from each verse of the Bible, surrounded by their team as they sought to translate God's Word into another language in Southeast Asia. They delighted in God's Word, and they felt His delight in them.

As Psalm 119 puts it,

I find my delight in your commandments,
    which I love.
I will lift up my hands toward your commandments,
    which I love,
    and I will meditate on your statutes. . . .

I open my mouth and pant,
> because I long for your commandments.

PSALM 119:47-48, 131, ESV

In life, we can lean with our time and hearts and minds toward many things. I can lean into my phone, lean into my child as I talk to him, or lean and rest my body on a sofa. Spiritually, we need to lean toward hearing from God through the pages of Scripture, hopefully with a hot coffee beside us as we intentionally spend time seeking the Lord. Taking the time to observe the text means we understand that we are looking for what God said to the original audience so we understand what God is saying to us. We seek to know *God*, not what we want Him to say in order to fit our own agendas. We are not reading the Bible to back up with Scripture our already-made decisions. We are seeking to get to know the *who* behind it all: our Creator, the One who delights in us. As we pour our hearts and minds into the pages of Scripture, we will see how God inclines His ear to us and leans into those who fear Him.

Did you know that plants and trees often grow toward the direction of light from a window? There is a scientific term for this: *phototropism*. "Trees do not sense which way is up; rather, their growth follows the direction from which light comes. This phenomenon is called phototropism, which means bending toward the light."[2] Let's keep an awareness of God always at the forefront of our minds—bending toward His delight, growing toward the light of His love.

No Substitute for the Word of God

I often use Instacart to order groceries for our family of seven, but it's not without its drama and sometimes it's a gamble. One day, unbeknownst to me, one of my sons (who was five at the time) took my phone and ordered three hundred dollars' worth of groceries.

When the deliveryman arrived and began to unload the many bags, I protested, "Uh, I did not order all these items."

From behind me, a little voice proudly announced, "I did!"

We had hilarious food that week: three bags of apples, two bottles of orange juice, Dunkin' K-Cups that my son had thought were donuts. He couldn't have been happier. Me . . . not so much.

And the other day, I was planning to have friends over for a barbecue. I ordered a bunch of burgers, buns, and extras for the meal. When I got my Instacart order, I noticed that instead of sixteen burgers, there were only four. So what had the Instacart employee decided to give me instead? He decided that a rotisserie chicken would work nicely along with an apple pie. The problem was that one of my guests was allergic to chicken, and I don't like storebought apple pie. I will never know for sure what happened there.

When we are on the chase for meaning in our lives, we usually head for the things we can reach easily to while away time—and often this means a big screen on the wall with endless shows or the phones in our hands. Just like the apple pie and the chicken were no substitute for the burgers I'd ordered, temporary distractions are no substitute for the Word of God. There is no greater wisdom, no more concrete foundation, no more excellent pursuit, no more sure promise. There is no better way to glean understanding and meaning.

One of the primary ways I have grown to love God is through reading Scripture. Yet throughout the Bible we see Satan's agenda to keep us confused about God's Word. This is evident in the biblical account of Jesus being tested in the wilderness in Luke 4:1-13:

> Jesus, full of the Holy Spirit, left the Jordan and was led
> by the Spirit into the wilderness, where for forty days he

was tempted by the devil. He ate nothing during those
days, and at the end of them he was hungry.
VERSES 1-2

The Holy Spirit led Jesus into the wilderness, into the chaos.
Jesus went into a season of testing, yet what we get to observe in
this passage is how important it is during a time of trial or testing to know the Word of God in context. This has been apparent
in my own life throughout unexpected loss, cross-cultural moves,
unforeseen illness, and challenging family relationships. Let's look
at how Satan tries to sow doubt in the Word of God:

The devil said to him, "If you are the Son of God, tell
this stone to become bread."
Jesus answered, "It is written: 'Man shall not live on
bread alone.'"
The devil led him up to a high place and showed him
in an instant all the kingdoms of the world. And he said
to him, "I will give you all their authority and splendor; it
has been given to me, and I can give it to anyone I want
to. If you worship me, it will all be yours."
Jesus answered, "It is written: 'Worship the Lord your
God and serve him only.'"
The devil led him to Jerusalem and had him stand on
the highest point of the temple. "If you are the Son of
God," he said, "throw yourself down from here. For it is
written:

"'He will command his angels concerning you
    to guard you carefully;
they will lift you up in their hands,
    so that you will not strike your foot against a stone.'"

Jesus answered, "It is said: 'Do not put the Lord your God to the test.'"

When the devil had finished all this tempting, he left him until an opportune time.

VERSES 3-13

In this passage, Jesus responds to temptation with Scripture: "It is written . . ." But guess what the devil does? He replies back with Scripture and says the exact same thing: "It is written." The devil is sneaky. He uses this opportunity to misuse and misinterpret God's words. He plucks a couple verses out of their context and misuses those verses in a way that was not intended. Many will declare, "It is written," but the important thing is knowing *why* and *how* it was written. What was the original intent? This passage helps us to understand some important hermeneutical principles: Scripture will never contradict Scripture, and it should not be taken out of context.

The crazy part about all of this is that in verses 10 and 11 the devil quotes Psalm 91. Psalm 91 is about God's protection for the one who trusts in the Lord. The devil is basically saying, "Throw yourself down—disobey God—but don't worry, God promises to protect you!" But as we know, even when we trust in God, life is full of perils, sufferings, and pitfalls. This verse cannot be used as a guarantee that nothing will ever go wrong in our lives. If we know the message of the Bible as a whole, we'll know that it has a lot to say about suffering and difficulties. We cannot pluck one verse out and ignore the rest of Scripture, which reveals to us that God is with us in the midst of our suffering, that suffering and difficulties have a purpose, and that God can use these things for our good (see 2 Corinthians 1:3-5).

Alfred Tennyson, an English poet, once wrote, "A lie which is all a lie may be met and fought with outright, / But a lie which is part a truth is a harder matter to fight."[3] Satan—the author of confusion—tries to sow doubt in the Word of God and tries to alter its meaning and cover up its truth and power.

Many times in my life, I have turned to the Bible when I've reached the end of my knowledge on a subject. Acknowledging my own limits has driven me again and again to the pages of Scripture. In the place of not knowing what to do next, God's Word has guided me toward wisdom. As Luke 11:28 says, "Blessed rather are those who hear the word of God and obey it." There is so much blessing from taking in God's Word and obeying it. Isaiah 40:8 says the Word of God will never perish: "The grass withers and the flowers fall, but the word of our God endures forever."

Firm Foundation

"Turn off at this exit," my husband directed. "Just for a minute," he quickly added. "I want you to see a foundation I poured." My husband is a builder and owns a foundation company. I have often joked with him about how the foundation of a house is no longer visible once the house is built on it. There really is not much to see, as all his hard work gets buried. Underneath every beautiful home is a foundation that was labored over.

Before my husband and I were married, we were both part of a mission trip to Guatemala. He had just established a board of directors for an orphanage in the mountains of Guatemala with a few other men, but they needed a building. Our mission team started with the foundation. It was hard work, but I knew that although it would not be visible for long, it was important work. We needed a strong foundation for when the winds, earthquakes, and rains beat down on the property. Matthew 7:24 says, "Therefore everyone who hears these words of mine and puts them into practice is like a wise man who built his house on the rock."

Just like we need a strong foundation for buildings, we also need a strong foundation that is built on truth for our lives. This starts with understanding what the Bible actually says—and receiving the tools to discern what that is. All those years, it's not that I wasn't doing Bible study right—it's just that I did not know that it could be richer, more fruitful, and even *more* exciting than I had ever experienced.

Before I started Bible college, I had always jumped right into applying the text to myself, skipping over all the other steps. Inductive Bible Study reoriented my perspective—I realized that first I needed to ask questions about the text. I needed to seek out the original intent of the Author before applying it to my life. It is easy to see a passage of Scripture and try to use it right away. It is much harder to first try to find out what we learn about God through the passage. What does it show us about His character? Through the Inductive Bible Study method, we learn how to ask questions of the text to grow in our knowledge of God. In the next chapter, we'll look at one of the most exciting ideas behind Inductive Bible Study: that the Bible is all one big story planned out by God from beginning to end.

DISCOVER THE BIGGER STORY
OF THE BIBLE

WHEN I WAS GROWING UP in Chiang Mai, Thailand, our weekly
worship service was at an international church that met on Sundays
in the late afternoon. When the service concluded, we often went
to the night bazaar to get dinner. The night bazaar is Chiang Mai's
vibrant evening market, which likely rivals any other in the world.
Our preferred place to eat was the Galare Food Court, a menagerie
of food stalls offering a wide variety of choices. During these hot,
sticky nights, my friends and I wolfed down plates of delicious
Thai food on top of a heap of white rice shaped like an upside-
down bowl. My favorite dish was *khao man gai tawt* (chicken with
rice) paired with Thai lemon iced tea. We finished it off with des-
sert: Thailand's most delicious mango sticky rice! If you've never
had it, trust me—it's amazing!

Once dinner was finished, it was time to stroll around the night bazaar. Twinkle lights danced along the path. The air was filled with the noise of haggling over prices and the smell of knockoff perfumes. The small kiosks displayed a wide variety of treasures: souvenirs, clothing, crafts, spices, glassware—and much to my dad's chagrin, pirated films that cost less than a dollar. If you've ever watched a pirated film, you know they are nothing like the real thing. The pirated films we purchased at the night bazaar were often filmed on a camcorder by someone who sneaked into the movie while it was in theaters. A pirated movie was only a distorted duplicate of the real thing. We would squint to make out the grainy video, sometimes blocked by a head bobbing up and down. We'd strain our ears to hear the muffled audio through the background noise of someone chomping popcorn. My dad, ever a man of integrity, did not want us to use our baht (Thai currency) to buy these movies. But much to his dismay, we couldn't resist.

Like an inferior copy of a movie, a spiritual diet made up only of other people's words, sermons, and takes on different Bible verses is grainy at best and doesn't live up to the real experience of engaging with the Bible for ourselves. Although it is wise to use biblical commentaries and scholars to guide us in reading the Word, it is also important that we read the Word ourselves. Looking to people far smarter than we are when we are beginning Bible study helps us to stay rooted in the truths of Scripture and guides us in our study. This can help

The most remarkable story in history is waiting to be discovered by each of us.

us avoid error. But have we become a generation that is okay with just settling for someone else's take? In this age, with so many resources available to us, we can spend our entire lives living off other people's views on the Scriptures. But why not just purchase the ticket and go see the real movie? Instead of settling for someone else's view, why not open our Bibles, read the story, dig into the details, and allow God to speak to our hearts? Let's not settle for a cheap camcorder viewing of God's Word from TikTok, Instagram, or other social media sound bites. The most remarkable story in history is waiting to be discovered by each of us. We just need to take the time and do the digging.

Diving into the Metanarrative

The story of the Bible begins with Creation and takes us all the way to the new heaven and earth, with the life, death, and resurrection of God's Son as the climax. At the beginning of time, Adam and Eve's sin caused a fatal fall that has impacted every human being. But God's plan could not be thwarted, and that plan included His only Son coming to earth, living a sinless life, and becoming the perfect sacrifice for our sins. Through Jesus' crucifixion and defeat of death, God redeemed what Adam and Eve had done. The Bible is the story of God's glory, His reign, and His never-ending Kingdom. In the end, sin and death will be gone, God's Kingdom will be everlasting, and His children will spend eternity with Him.

This big, overarching story of the Bible is called the metanarrative. When we study a passage of Scripture, it's important to understand not only its historical context and how it fits into the chapter and the book it's in, but also how it fits into the metanarrative—the story that remains unified from Genesis to Revelation.

I was chatting with a friend the other day, and the word *spirit* came up—as in, I mentioned that she had a genuine spirit about her. She asked me to explain what I meant by "genuine spirit." I realized I didn't know how to explain it in easy terms. There are many words and phrases in the English language that are difficult to explain. Similarly, if you have ever attempted to describe the storyline of the Bible in your own words from beginning to end, you might find yourself stumbling. Details become murky, and suddenly you wonder—as you trip over your words—whether you are getting the story right.

In the field of Bible translation, a method is available to help translators stay focused on the big picture of the Bible's story. Before they dive deep into translation work, they use a tool called storying. Storying involves telling Bible stories in your own words before you go about translating them into another language. This is a familiar way of working in most cultures of the world, which already use oral storytelling. Often, spoken word stories are a primary way of passing down information to the next generation.

Think about it: Have you ever heard a story from a friend and then repeated the story to another person later? After listening to a story, and then sharing the story with someone else, you may begin to internalize it. Maybe you even catch additional details that you missed when you were told the story the first time—as your memory begins to rehash what was said.

It's the same with translation. When a translator internalizes a story, they're better able to translate it because they understand it as part of a bigger narrative. Translating it becomes less about regurgitating the passage word for word and more about developing the passage within the context of the larger story.

What about when we just read Scripture for ourselves? We begin to internalize its messages as we read. We further internalize them when we tell others about what we have read. Part of internalizing is knowing where a passage of Scripture fits in the metanarrative.

The biblical metanarrative is comprised of four parts: Creation, Fall, Redemption, and Restoration. The details will make more sense when we keep the whole story in view. Just like zooming in on a painting's details shows us the intricacies of the brushstrokes, zooming out shows us the grand design. When we read the Bible, we want to consider its different books, of course, but we also need to understand how they all fit together.

Creation: Creation is the beginning of the grand metanarrative. God brought order to chaos and formed the void into His good creation. He then created people in His image and declared that they were "very good" (Genesis 1:31). Man and woman would live in perfect harmony alongside each other in God's Kingdom. The world was at peace. Humans were meant for enjoying the presence of God and serving willingly under His kingship, stewards over the animals, the land, and the whole created order.

Fall: The fall of man is the major conflict in this metanarrative. In Genesis 3, Adam and Eve rejected God's rule. Sin entered the world: men and women were separated from God and became enemies of God and in conflict with each other. Death and destruction came into the picture. Yet even in the midst of this tragedy, we hear the beginning of good news and hints of a coming resolution. It is here we see the first gospel, the *protoevangelium*:

> I will put enmity between you and the woman,
>   and between your offspring and her offspring;
> he shall bruise your head,
>   and you shall bruise his heel.
> GENESIS 3:15, ESV

This verse (Genesis 3:15) gives a glimpse of hope for mankind. God promises, right from the start, that one day a descendant of Eve will come and defeat the devil. That hope—which was fulfilled through the person of Christ—shows us that God still reigns and His plans will not be stopped.

Redemption: God's redemption story is the peak of the narrative! God loved us so much that He had compassion on us (see John 3:16). The death and resurrection of our Savior, Jesus Christ, was God's big redeeming plan all along. We can now be reconciled with God and become His friends (see John 15:14-15) and as a result with the Holy Spirit's presence we can learn how to love one another. He offers forgiveness and rescues us from our sins. Once we realize the whole Bible points to this climax, we begin to see how much redemption is woven throughout the Scriptures.

Restoration: In every good story, the writer seeks to have a gripping ending. Restoration is that ending for the metanarrative of the Scriptures. We live in the already-but-not-yet tension now, so the final restoration at the Lord's second coming is something we look toward with great anticipation. The Lord—the great writer of the story—has given us a peek into its ending. Jesus rules today, and He has already defeated sin through His death on the cross. One day He will return and rule in fullness. The world will be renewed, and everything will be restored. Jesus will put an end to evil—once and for all.

Noticing Overarching Themes

One big part of biblical theology is tracing themes through the metanarrative. Enclyclopedia.com defines a theme as "an idea that recurs in or pervades a work of art or literature."[1]

As you read the Bible, you'll notice certain themes developing in both the Old Testament and the New. As an article from Zondervan.com points out, "Biblical theology traces the themes that run through Scripture as they were progressively revealed through time."[2]

Imagine that you are reading your Bible and you notice a

certain important idea. For example, maybe you see that a section of Scripture mentions the Kingdom of God, blessing and curse, exile, or heaven and earth. Then you turn to a different book of the Bible and notice the same ideas there. You diligently take out your highlighters and begin to mark the key words you find. Soon you feel you have discovered a theme connecting those two books. It's exciting to find themes that are new to you.

Finding a theme in the Bible leads you closer to finding the purpose behind the words written. It leads you to the why or the intent of the storyline. It helps you to grasp the overarching story and understand what you are reading. Did you know there are tools to help you continue to search for a specific theme? You can try to find that same theme in the rest of the pages of Scripture by using certain software. I typically use Logos Bible Software to do this. To start, I search the key words that surround a theme and see if they come up in other books of the Bible. Similarly, I was taught by Nancy Guthrie that you can use the ESV app to search for different themes and then explore each of the verses you find them in. As a reminder, it's important not to take verses out of their context. Make sure to read the passage that surrounds a verse in order to understand what the theme of the verse looks like in context.

At this point, you can also ask yourself questions about the metanarrative. *How does the theme that I found fit into the four stages of the grand story of the Bible? What does it look like to trace a specific theme through the metanarrative as a whole?*

It is easy to see a theme run through a movie or book. We are taught to look for themes like love, friendship, courage, and even good versus evil in different forms of literature or movies. We can do the same thing when we're studying the Bible! When we learn that the Greek words for *joy* or *rejoice* are used sixteen times in the book of Philippians, we might consider that rejoicing is one of the book's themes.[3] Another way to look for themes is by trying to find an area where the author explains the purpose for writing the text. Sometimes it is stated in the introduction of a Bible book; in other cases it is included in the closing statements. And sometimes it stands alone!

The fact that you can find themes woven throughout the Bible—from Genesis to Revelation—is a beautiful example of the unity of Scripture. Think about the themes of light and darkness or blessing and curse. You will find themes like these in most books of the Bible. Although different authors wrote these books at different times, the same God was giving them the words, so the metanarrative's threads remain consistent.

> *The fact that you can find themes woven throughout the Bible is a beautiful example of the unity of Scripture.*

Christ is the most important thread of the metanarrative. We can see Him no matter what part of the Bible we're reading. By the time my younger children arrived, someone brilliant invented a pacifier that glowed. I no longer had to grope around in the dark when they lost their pacifier at night—I immediately saw a tiny glowing ember in their room. Like that beacon of light in the darkness, Christ now leaps out at me in every page of Scripture I read. As I grow older and more mature in my walk with the Lord, I see Jesus not only in explicitly gospel-centric passages but also typified in the characters of Adam, Joseph, Moses, and others. (*Typify* just means "to serve as a symbol or emblem of; symbolize; prefigure."[4])

I now understand that the Old Testament foreshadows Jesus' coming in the New Testament and that Old Testament prophecy and typology are fulfilled in Christ's work. All of history found its hope in Jesus Christ crucified. He is the climax of all of Scripture. If you're looking for the redemptive story of God, Christ is at the center of it: "The more common approach to understanding the redemptive nature of all biblical texts is to identify how God's Word *predicts, prepares for, reflects,* or *results from* the person and/ or work of Christ."[5]

Pantry Dump

My friend Shauna is quite the chef. I love going to her house to experience her delicious cooking. One day she brought an impressive-looking salad to our small group get-together, and we all asked for the recipe. It was so colorful and healthy, and it had so many different types of greens and veggies in it. Her response was, "It's a pantry dump."

I could not help but tease her. If I were doing a pantry dump, you would find some stale crackers, a can of year-old chicken noodle soup that I forgot about, and maybe a sweet potato that was sprouting legs. You definitely would not be able to string together a beautiful salad! Fortunately, if Scripture were a pantry, it would look more like Shauna's than mine. When we read the Bible, we aren't creating a new interpretation. We are working with the riches that are already available to us in the text. When we put together all the parts of Scripture, including its various themes, literary genres, and sections, we are left with a cohesive and impressive pantry dump. All the pieces fit into one big recipe, or grand story of redemption. Later on, we will learn how to interpret these pieces in and of themselves. Before we get to that, I want to spend some time discussing the difficult but important subject of how to detect false teaching.

4

RECOGNIZE FALSE TEACHING

CROSS-CULTURAL MOVES come with their fair share of confusing situations. As a missionary kid, not only was I not up to date on pop culture and clothing trends, but I also had a hard time understanding English slang and idioms. In order to determine some of the definitions, I had to rely heavily on the context. In college, I was asked on a date. The day came, and I got a text from the young man that said, "Could I get a rain check? I have a big paper due tomorrow." I did not understand what *rain check* meant, so I thought long and hard about the context. I went to the window to check for rain, but there was none. Finally, I asked a friend what it meant. After she explained the term, I realized that it made sense given the context of the message.

Consider the Context

When we look at a verse out of context, it's easy to misinterpret it, or even fall prey to false teaching. That is why I suggest that the first thing you do before you deep-dive into any passage of Scripture is read through the whole book, or at least the surrounding passages, a few times. It's a good idea to read the verses once out loud too. When we seek to understand a verse's context, we subscribe to the idea that the Bible has order, that the syntax (arrangement of words, phrases, and sentences) was purposefully derived.

When we think about interpreting an epistle, for example, we must keep in mind that it was originally a letter, that there were no paragraph breaks or chapter headings in the original version (like an email you and I would read today)—and that it was often read aloud to an audience. When we consider the context of the Gospels, we understand that the writers were detailing events and retelling parables that are not primarily organized chronologically, but instead thematically. Although they follow a general chronological order, they do not reference time the way we do today. It is important to always keep in mind the themes, the purpose of the author, and the audience as we read each Gospel. When we think through a historical narrative (the Pentateuch or the book of Acts, for instance), we must understand that these books are told as stories. If we were to isolate a passage in the middle of a book, we might not understand why Saul was chasing David, what Esther's background was, or how Ruth and Naomi were related. The surrounding passages hold crucial details for understanding the meaning of the passage.

It's not always easy to interpret Scripture within the larger context. The truth is, while we are told that context is key and that we need to search for "the plain meaning of the text," this is more easily said than done. Aren't we always trying to interpret the meaning correctly? How about when we all try to do this and come up with different conclusions? I have seen well-meaning Christians fall into the trap of reading verses in ways that are misconstrued.

This means that the first appropriate response to a misinterpretation of Scripture is grace. All of us need help understanding what we are reading from time to time. Desiring to read Scripture responsibly does not undermine the power of the Spirit to work in and through the text, making it come alive for the believer. Still, we can practice good stewardship by learning as much as we can about biblical literacy. We should understand that when we read Scripture, we bring our own perspectives and life circumstances to the pages, which means we must approach it with humility. Two people can read the same passage yet come to different conclusions about the text because of cultural context or time in history. We can be well-meaning in our interpretation and still make mistakes. I know I have!

The first appropriate response to a misinterpretation of Scripture is grace.

To further illustrate this point, we must ask the question: How can the prosperity gospel movement, the Word of Faith movement, and other false gospels be reading the same Bible that we read? You see, the prosperity gospel often interprets verses incorrectly because it ignores the literary or cultural-historical context. The prosperity gospel might quote a verse on wealth, riches, or favor without regard for the surrounding text. A well-known example is John 14:12, 14, where Jesus says, "Very truly I tell you, whoever believes in me will do the works I have been doing, and they will do even greater things than these, because I am going to the Father. . . . You may ask me for anything in my name, and I will do it." Adherents to the prosperity gospel believe that verse 12 means Jesus' disciples will do more powerful miracles and more sensational things than Christ Himself. Verse 14 is misunderstood to say that we can ask for anything in Jesus' name (material blessings, health, money, etc.) and it will be granted to us.

Now let's look at how each of these verses *should* be interpreted. Again, I urge you to read the entire chapter of John 14 for context. Jesus has gathered His faithful followers together before His death to speak to them. In verse 12, when He mentions "greater things," He is referencing the fact that His disciples will spread the gospel farther and expand the church throughout the world—for example, when three thousand people come to know Christ through Peter's sermon (see Acts 2:41). But the key to all this growth is Christ. The proof for this reading of the text is in the pudding. No human has done more powerful or miraculous works than Christ did Himself, but we have seen the gospel spread much farther than it did in Jesus' day.

Verse 14 is often misconstrued to mean that God will give us whatever we ask for, but based on our experience and the message of the Bible as a whole, we also know this is not correct. The key here is "in my name," which means in line with the character of Jesus. In context, we read the statement as reassurance Jesus gave to the disciples before He ascended to heaven. The disciples would face great uncertainty, and Jesus was reminding them that they could always cry out to Him and call on His name.

When we talk about Bible study, it is so important to discuss how to handle the Word of God with the utmost care. From the very beginning of the early church, false teachers arose. In fact, Paul addresses false teaching and misunderstanding about the gospel in almost all of his letters. Since so much of the New Testament addresses false teaching, this should make us cautious about how we study the Word and whom we listen to. Here are some good examples in Galatians of the kind of false teaching the early church faced: "Some false believers had infiltrated our ranks to spy on the freedom we have in Christ Jesus and to make us slaves" (2:4).

These teachers were telling all new Christian converts, including Gentiles, that they had to be circumcised, even as Christians. They had even convinced Peter to avoid eating with Gentiles! As Paul wrote, "Those people are zealous to win you over, but for no good. What they want is to alienate you from us, so that you may have zeal for them. It is fine to be zealous, provided the purpose is good, and to be so always, not just when I am with you" (4:17-18). Often false teachers are very sincere, and it's easy to be influenced by their passion. I have seen my fair share of enthusiastic false teaching over the years—teachers who are passionate, convincing, and charismatic. I have had direct confrontations with some who distort the true gospel, and because of these experiences I have learned a few helpful ways to spot a false teacher—and to explain to someone else how the teacher is mishandling the Word of God.

Descriptive versus Prescriptive

Many teachers—whether false or not—mishandle God's Word because they do not understand the difference between descriptive texts and prescriptive texts. When we come to a passage of Scripture, it's important that we make this distinction. A descriptive passage details an event and describes what happened. A prescriptive passage tells someone what to do, when to do it, or what should happen.

When my kids and I read history books, we get a descriptive account of a certain time in the past. If we read a book about Paul Revere warning the people that the British were coming, we would not assume that we must ride horseback at midnight and eat and dress as Paul Revere did. We would be inspired by his courage, enthusiasm, and bravery, but we would not read this type of book for advice on how to live. We can most definitely learn from stories, but they are not meant to be instructions.

When I tell my kids they should wash their hands before dinner and inform my boys that showering just once every ten days is not acceptable, I am instructing them in life and godliness. *Ahem,* I mean in *personal hygiene.* I do not explain to my boys that they must shower more than once a week by telling them a descriptive story about how I used to bathe in the river in my village on the border of Thailand and Myanmar. I do not tell them about how I remember stepping on elephant dung every time I stepped into the water (true story!). Instead, I prescriptively tell them they must shower unless they want to scare away all the boys and girls in their class. Not to mention their future girlfriends.

Some false teachers will tell people that the book of Acts is prescriptive in its explanation of salvation: that is, that salvation comes by copying the steps outlined in Acts 2:38. But theologians agree that the book of Acts is best understood as a descriptive recounting of the history of the early church. The theological elements of the book of Acts need to be considered in light of what Luke, the author, was trying to communicate to his audience. In seeking to find the purpose of the book of Acts, we must understand that Luke was primarily telling the story of the church.

Other times false teachers misunderstand genre. They read *one* book of the Bible and create a theology based solely on this historical narrative. We will go deeper into the importance of genre later in this book, but for now, consider that a false teacher might interpret the book of Acts to mean that Christians today must do everything the way the early church did.

If we are trying to model what the book of Acts imparts to us, we need to do it in a broader sense by learning from the overall purpose of the book. Let's consider how theologians Gordon Fee and Douglas Stuart address the idea of understanding the larger sense of the book of Acts: "Luke . . . probably intended that the ongoing church should be 'like them,' but in the larger sense of proclaiming the good news to the entire world, not by modeling itself on any specific example."[1]

Again, Acts is describing the early church at a certain point in history, not prescribing how all churches must function in future millennia. If the book of Acts were prescriptive, then we would need to set it up as a pattern for all things. Fee and Stuart go on to state the following:

> The crucial hermeneutical question here is whether biblical narratives that describe what happened in the early church also function as norms intended to delineate what should or must happen in the ongoing church. Are there instances from Acts of which one may appropriately say, "We must do this," or should one merely say, "We may do this"? Our assumption, shared by many others, is this: Unless Scripture explicitly tells us we must do something, what is only narrated or described does not function in a normative (i.e., obligatory) way—unless it can be demonstrated on other grounds that the author intended it to function in this way.[2]

Many false teachers have great zeal and even good intentions. Some might argue that the church today has lost *its* zeal and needs to be more like the first-century Christians. They could be zealous to restore passion to the church, and this can all come from a good place. But let's keep discussing the book of Acts, since it is often misinterpreted. Instead of reading the book of Acts as a historical narrative and primarily an account of how the gospel spread from Jews to Gentiles, a false teacher may take a descriptive passage of Scripture and make it prescriptive. It is easy to get these confused since the Bible does contain many prescriptive teaching passages. However, these all make it clear that salvation is a gift of grace through faith alone (see John 5:24 and 11:25-26; Romans 10:9; Ephesians 1:13-14). Unlike these verses, Acts 2:38 is not intended as a foundational verse on which to develop a theology of salvation. We must read this verse—and the book of Acts as a whole—in light of all of God's Word.

If these teachers took the rest of Scripture into account, they would see that salvation is not a multistep formula, and water baptism is not necessary to be saved. Belief in Christ is sufficient. The context of the whole canon of Scripture is necessary for accurate biblical interpretation. As Paul said to the Ephesian elders, "I did not shrink from declaring to you the whole counsel of God" (Acts 20:27, ESV). A book of the Bible cannot be separated from the rest of Scripture.

Progressive Revelation

I find it interesting that God reveals Himself gradually through the pages of Scripture, a process known as progressive revelation. [3] In the Old Testament, the Israelites did not have the Messiah yet—only prophecies about the Messiah to come. As we read through the Bible, we watch progressive revelation unfold: God chooses ancient Israel to be His people, and then all the promises He gives them find their fulfillment years later in Jesus Christ. The redemptive truth of the metanarrative or overarching story of the Bible unfolds as we read, and the means by which God is going to save His people becomes evident as we get further into the pages of Scripture.

One of the clearest ways I see progressive revelation in the Bible is through the sacrificial system. In the Old Testament, the blood of animal sacrifice was necessary to atone for the Israelites' sins.

Once we arrive at the New Testament, we see that Christ is the all-sufficient sacrifice for sin and that animal sacrifices are no longer necessary. As the book of Hebrews says, "It is not possible for the blood of bulls and goats to take away sins" (10:4, NLT), meaning the Old Testament sacrificial system did not provide permanent cleansing. Much of the mystery and foreshadowing of the Old Testament becomes clear in the New.

When we read the Bible, we need to keep an eye out for God's progressive revelation. The Israelites' experience in the Old Testament gives us a sense of how God might move amid His people today, but we must also remember what we know of God through the New Testament.

I often like to say that the Old Testament red-carpets the New Testament. In other words, it lays out prophecies and promises that are then fulfilled at the end of the red carpet by Jesus Christ. The Old and New Testaments are equally inspired and valuable, but we see God reveal more and more of Himself over time as we read the Bible from beginning to end. The book of Acts serves as a bridge between the Gospels and the Epistles. For example, we can find information on the beginnings of the church of Philippi in the book of Acts, and then go on to the Epistles to find Paul's letter to the Philippians.

As we read through the Gospels, the book of Acts, and the Epistles, our understanding of our relationship with God grows. In the Old Testament we see God the Father interacting with His people, then we see Jesus incarnate on earth, and then in the Epistles we see so many examples of what it means to be united with Christ, Christ in us. Most of Paul's arguments have to do with our unity with Christ, Christ dwelling within us. For example, Galatians 2:20 says, "I have been crucified with Christ. It is no longer I who live, but Christ who lives in me" (ESV).

The Primary Purpose

The way we interpret the book of Acts can be complicated. Many believers come to the book desiring to emulate the signs and wonders they see. The apostolic age was exciting because Jesus had risen from the dead and ascended to heaven, the Holy Spirit had come to reside in all believers, and the church was growing and spreading from Jerusalem to Rome. But we cannot just pluck out one verse from the book of Acts about salvation and the Holy Spirit without examining the context of what all the other Scriptures say. This is such an important truth when we study the Bible. Some teachers will focus only on the words of Jesus or ignore the Old Testament. When someone teaches the Bible like that, we should question whether what is taught is truth.

Many believers, too, want to model their lives after the early church. If the early church looked a certain way in its passion for Jesus and the Christian life, why shouldn't we? I, for one, understand why this is a huge draw. In many ways we should seek to imitate the early church—in its generosity, prayerfulness, desire to utilize spiritual gifts (see Acts 2:42-47), and eagerness to understand the Scriptures. We read in Acts that the Berean Jews were of "noble character" and received the gospel message with "great eagerness." Let's read the verse in full:

> The Berean Jews were of more noble character than those in Thessalonica, for they received the message with great eagerness and examined the Scriptures every day to see if what Paul said was true.
> ACTS 17:11

I read verses like this about the early church and am rightfully inspired! It can be a good thing to find inspiration in historical examples. And these examples of the early church's lifestyle are backed up by other Scriptures that urge us to have attitudes like those believers'. Yet we cannot seek to normalize or establish a pattern for our churches that exactly copies what happened in the book of Acts or we would all have tongues of fire over our heads (see Acts 2:3)! Should every church choose seven men to serve food to widows at the church (6:1-6)? Should we all expect that, like Stephen, we will see heaven opened and witness Jesus at God's right hand (7:56)? And should our church leaders reside in Jerusalem (8:1)? I don't think so!

Instead of coming to the book of Acts with preconceived notions of what we want to discover, we must understand what the author, Luke, hoped to impart to his readers. In order to do this practically, we need to examine the book as a whole. The first step is to contemplate Luke's desire for writing the book. No matter which book of the Bible you're reading, it will take work to discover the author's intent and the book's general themes, but these steps will enrich your study. I am by no means saying that you must come to an understanding independently; I encourage you always to check your interpretations with biblically based scholars. I recommend Logos Bible Software to anyone and everyone, and I am including an appendix of additional helpful resources in the back of this book.

Let us acknowledge together that the book of Acts and all the other books of the New Testament were not written as isolated units. No book is an island. Acts directly follows the book of Luke; it has continuous momentum and a continuous theological message. The book of Luke offers us a vision of the spread of the gospel after Christ's life, death, and resurrection. Then, in the book of Acts, we learn of His ascension and the growth of the church. When we understand the big picture of Luke and Acts, Luke's primary purpose of recording all that Jesus taught before

His death, followed by a record of the early church's activities, comes into focus.

The Already-but-Not-Yet Kingdom

Our questions about the future can be another stumbling block as we seek to pursue sound biblical interpretation and avoid false teaching. What can we expect from this life, and what is reserved for the new heavens and the new earth? Were certain prophecies fulfilled by Christ's coming, or are they yet to be fulfilled? When biblical texts get misconstrued, it's often because we have too much of a desire for heaven to be on earth and for all of God's promises to be fulfilled now. We know Jesus' reign has already been inaugurated, but what does it look like to live with the tension of the now and not yet? We must embrace the fact that in this life God can heal, but He might not always choose to heal. Yet in heaven we will see that "he will wipe every tear from their eyes. There will be no more death or mourning or crying or pain, for the old order of things has passed away" (Revelation 21:4). Our hope for wholeness is waiting for us in heaven: "Praise be to the God and Father of our Lord Jesus Christ! In his great mercy he has given us new birth into a living hope through the resurrection of Jesus Christ from the dead, and into an inheritance that can never perish, spoil or fade. This inheritance is kept in heaven for you" (1 Peter 1:3-4). During our lives on earth, we can enjoy the past, present, and future hope of sanctification—and begin enjoying life with Christ on the throne now.

In the world around us, we will see and hear false teaching on social media, on TV, in churches, and at other gatherings. That is why I feel it is so important to learn how to study and understand the Scriptures. I can see why most of Paul's letters to the churches involve correcting false doctrine, uprooting heresy, and defending the one true gospel. As he says in Philippians, "It is right for me to feel this way about you all, because I hold you in my heart, for you are all partakers with me of grace, both in my imprisonment and in the defense and confirmation of the gospel" (1:7, ESV). Paul takes any distortion of the gospel very seriously. If someone preaches a "different gospel," he says, the true gospel is emptied of its power. Paul writes to the Galatian church, "I am amazed how quickly you are deserting the One who called you by the grace of Christ and are turning to a different gospel—which is not even a gospel. Evidently some people are troubling you and trying to distort the gospel of Christ" (Galatians 1:6-7, BSB).

The Scriptures make clear that we are new creatures in Christ, and we are meant to bear fruit. Many false teachers today focus on signs and wonders (power, healing, tongues, casting out demons, miraculous phenomena). Often it is because they take a verse or a passage out of context or use descriptive passages as though they're prescriptive. Once we learn the importance of taking into account all of Scripture—including the context of passages and books, as well as whether those passages are prescriptive or descriptive— we will begin to discern whether there is error in the teachings we hear. People are drawn to signs and wonders, and I believe God can perform miracles for His glory if He so desires. Still, the less exciting—but ultimately more important—focus throughout Scripture is the fruit of loving God, loving the people around us, and becoming more like Christ.

A Change of Heart

One time, I was confronted with false teaching at a women's conference. I walked into a beautiful sanctuary with lights and decorations abounding. I took my seat next to a few other women, and smiling gingerly, we exchanged pleasantries.

"Where are you from?" I asked my neighbor.

"Florida," she whispered back as the music cued us to silence.

I sang loudly as I raised my hands in worship, and then the teaching began. As I listened intently to the words of the speaker, I began to stir. *Hmm . . . what is she saying? It sounds like she is misunderstanding the context of the passages she is preaching on . . .* Eventually, I grew so uncomfortable that I left. I sat in the nursing mothers' room and cried. The Lord had brought me to a conference full of teaching, worship, and fellowship. Yet when I got there and began to listen, the words spoken from the front were not biblically informed or sound. While I knew the Bible teacher wasn't intentionally seeking to mislead anyone, her explanation of Scripture was more like a glorified personal application full of theological misunderstandings. She was speaking some truth, but not the whole truth.

While it was not the moment to speak up or argue against what I was hearing, it made me genuinely sad. And my sadness really surprised me. It made me realize that the Lord had *changed my own heart for the better.* He had changed my heart from studying the Bible to prove a point to studying it because I loved God and others. For so long, when I knew I was right about something, I felt compelled to correct or teach. I wanted to prove I had what it took to be a Bible teacher. *I wanted to prove I was smart.* Yet, suddenly, while present at this conference, I went from sad to mad at God for letting His sheep be led astray. Suddenly I was pounding on heaven's door on behalf of these believers. I was asking God how He could allow teachers to mishandle His Word and let so many unaware believers sit under such destructive exposition of Scripture. My anger moved my heart to pray fervently. I was no longer writing rebuttals in my head, thinking about confronting the teacher, or talking *about* her to others, but I also wasn't lukewarm or apathetic. I still had the passion God had given me for His Word, but my concern was now coming from genuine love.

I realized where I had gotten it all wrong. Before, I did not have an earnest desire to equip the saints that sprang from heartfelt love. I was just plain puffed up, swollen with knowledge (see 1 Corinthians 8:1). Christians full of Bible knowledge but lacking in love remind me of a set of two balloons that were tangled in our chandelier for almost a year. They served no purpose because they rose to the height of our ceiling—an unreachable height—got snarled up, and eventually became an eyesore. We finally had to get a painter's ladder to take them down.

The Lord had changed my heart from studying the Bible to prove a point to studying it because I loved God and others.

Like those balloons, we can rise to the heights of biblical knowledge yet become unreachable to others, tangle ourselves in the web of our theology, and remain entirely separated from the people the Bible calls us to love. We can be so puffed up with knowledge that we forget what the Bible urges us to do. We might succumb to hanging out with only other believers or believers who think the same way we do about everything. We might forget that the Bible is meant to be heeded, and instead just be comfortable reading with little to no obedience involved.

While I was being deflated, the needle kind of hurt. But I wasn't focused only on being right anymore. I no longer asked God to use me and only me in this fight. I prayed that if the Lord would let me, I would love to serve Him, and if He would let me, I would love to come alongside people who wanted to grow in biblical literacy. I now desire for everyone to be passionate, confident, and excited about studying the Bible.

Reading in Context Leads to Transformation

Have you ever heard of Mehran Karimi Nasseri? He was an Iranian man who slept on an airport bench for eighteen years of his life. That wasn't his original plan—at first, he had a destination. He wanted to go to England to find his birth mother, but en route to England, he got lost in transit.

Nasseri ended up living in the Paris Charles de Gaulle airport for eighteen years. His journey (and life in the airport) inspired a book and two movies. Whether Nasseri was exiled from Iran for protests or whether he was fleeing political turmoil is unknown. He was never allowed to return home, but he did not have the proper identification papers to go elsewhere in Europe either. He found himself stateless and in limbo. No country would allow him to officially enter without proper identification, but France allowed him to live in their airport terminal. Finally, France granted him citizenship, but upon leaving the airport, he struggled to figure out his life beyond the terminal walls. He returned to the airport and died at gate 2F.[4]

What this story reminds me of is how we can get lost and end up in limbo instead of moving forward. I don't want this for you—or myself, for that matter. When it comes to reading Scripture, I don't want you to be discouraged by having to learn how to read with a new perspective. Ultimately, the Scriptures are not there to get us lost in technicalities or overwhelmed by where to begin. As we seek to learn about the Bible, let it lead us to worship God. My heart's desire for you would be that you would let the Spirit lead you in your study and let Him transform your heart as you seek to read the Scriptures with context and greater understanding. Do not let this new way of reading leave you homeless at gate 2F! Instead, reach toward this new destination with the Lord. You can even ask Him for guidance and clarity. Let Him mold and change your heart. Through this, I know you will learn more about Him in the process.

The book of Acts has quite a few themes we could run with—most books do! Am I proposing that we read the book of Acts only as a historical record, trying to leave out any personal response? No, not at all! I believe every part of the Bible serves a purpose for life, edifies the church body, and demonstrates God's plan and purposes. Many of the gospel proclamations in the book of Acts result in people repenting. "Luke in his two-volume work, Luke-Acts, emphasizes repentance more than any other NT author. Nearly one-half, or twenty-five of the fifty-eight uses of the primary NT terms for repentance (*metanoeo* and *metanoia*) occur in Luke-Acts."[5] As we meditate on this observation about repentance in Luke and Acts, may we humbly ask the Lord to change our hearts. Many people focus on the supernatural power demonstrated throughout the book of Acts and miss this theme of repentance.

Paul says, "And now I commend you to God and to the word of his grace, which is able to build you up and to give you the inheritance among all those who are sanctified" (Acts 20:32, ESV). In other words, once we have dug in deeply, there are so many takeaways from the book of Acts we can incorporate into our lives. Through this verse and others, we believe that Scripture is a word of grace meant to build us up. The book of Acts has taught me to be more generous and pray more boldly. I am comforted by the fact that the gospel spreads despite opposition and false teaching. There are countless principles that I can take from the book as a believer. I am comforted, encouraged, and spurred on by the book of Acts. The goal of all Scripture reading is transformation and intimacy with Christ. As you continue to learn about biblical literacy, can I urge you to stop and worship? The last thing I want for you is to be so puffed up with knowledge that you lack love— which is the reason behind all of this! May our hearts be softened to know and love our Savior more.

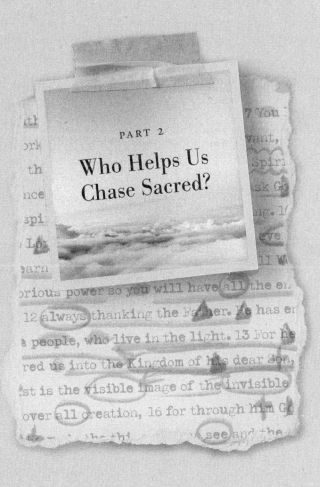

PART 2

Who Helps Us Chase Sacred?

THE ROLE OF THE SPIRIT

SIDE-BY-SIDES, DIRT BIKES, and four-wheelers have become my parental contribution to my current stage of life. I can run a diagnostic test as I start them, restart them, and bleed gasoline. We live in a small town in southern New Hampshire; many years ago, I did not realize how much I would enjoy the land surrounding our house. The boys and I regularly run our motorized vehicles, and we love exploring. The little pond in the back of our house is full of great critters. The beautiful black fountain that my husband strategically put in front of our home has become the spawning ground for thousands of frogs. I would not be surprised if we had a frog apocalypse where they all started beating down the door. You live in this small New Hampshire town for the land. It's also close to the mountains for hiking, and its four dramatic seasons come and go with everyone adding their two cents: "I do not remember a spring this rainy!" "The temps were frigid this year."

New England is famous for its quaint town centers. Ours has a white church with a graveyard and a few homes with candles flickering in the windows to warm the otherwise-dreary New England nights. There is a tradition in our town center that happens every year around Christmastime. The townspeople sing songs and light the Christmas tree, and Santa appears at the top of the bell tower, waving to all the children below.

This year, there was a sign with glowing letters that turned on at the same time as the Christmas tree. As we counted down to the grand reveal, the Christmas tree sparkled beautifully while the light-up sign struggled, flashed, and looked like it was on fire. Finally, a few words flickered on, and I could only make out Ha Ho. A large part of the Happy Holidays message did not light up at all! I always grin when I see a well-meaning restaurant sign where some letters have grown dim, and you are left to strain your eyes and try to decipher what it is supposed to say. Often, the brighter letters can make some hilarious sayings. Like when you go to a drive-thru and the *r* and *v* are dimmed, resulting in Die-Thru.

The Spirit Illuminates Scripture

Whenever I see these light-up signs, I am reminded of how the Spirit illuminates the Word of God for us (see 1 Corinthians 2:10-14)—and none of the letters of God's Word ever burn out. The words in the Bible feel like they jump off the page when the Holy Spirit convicts us of wrongdoing or reveals His truth in a fresh way. A certain word or phrase can sometimes seem to light up in a way that speaks to our deepest longings and heartaches. Scripture provides comfort in ways that no human words can. Its words are not dull but full of power and promise as the Spirit helps us to understand what is written in the pages (see John 16:13-15). The Bible is living and active, "sharper than any double-edged sword" (Hebrews 4:12). This means that the Bible teaches us what is good and what is evil. The Bible cuts away what is not of God. Through the work of the Holy Spirit, people are drawn to God through His Word, and His Word gives us the assurance our hearts long for. The Word of God gives us what Paul prays for the readers of Ephesians: "spiritual wisdom and insight so that you might grow in your knowledge of God. I pray that your hearts will be flooded with light so that you can understand the confident hope he has given to those he called—his holy people who are his rich and glorious inheritance" (Ephesians 1:17-18, NLT).

The work of the Spirit in and through the Bible helps us to discern truth and wisdom: "The unfolding of your words gives light; it gives understanding to the simple" (Psalm 119:130). The Spirit brings understanding to our Bible reading and helps us to apply our knowledge correctly. We know the Spirit also convicts us of sin through Scripture and can bring us to saving faith.

We also know that reading the Bible doesn't mean we will automatically understand it. We need the power of the Spirit, the power of prayer, and the power of sound study to help us correctly interpret the text. When the Pharisees wanted to trap Jesus by confusing Him with controversial religious topics, Jesus answered them, "Have you not read?"

> *The work of the Spirit in and through the Bible helps us to discern truth and wisdom.*

(Matthew 12:3, ESV). The Pharisees were extremely well educated, and yes, they knew their Scripture. But there was a gap between their knowledge and their understanding as well as between their knowledge and their hearts. They had not internalized what they'd learned, and their motive behind reading Scripture was off. Jesus answered the religious leaders quite a few times with "Have you not read?"

I imagine a lot of religious debates today would benefit from that simple question. If we spent more time in our Bibles and pursued wisdom, we would gain more clarity, not less. As logical and smart as these religious leaders thought they were, Jesus expected them to apply the answers from reading the inspired Word. Scripture is meant to be examined and studied (like the Bereans did in Acts 17:11) and applied in our everyday lives.

Sometimes we, like the Pharisees, go to the Bible with mixed motives. My friend recently said, "I did not feel God was near in my trials. But then again, it recently dawned on me that I did not want God's presence; I wanted God's plan. I kept asking when my trials would end." My friend wanted a blueprint for navigating her challenging circumstances. When could she expect to be finished with the difficulties she was having? Many of us have a desire similar to hers—we want a blueprint for our individual lives. Sometimes when we approach the Bible with this single-minded goal, we are met with much more depth than we anticipated. We are met with relationship.

We often approach the Bible because we want to know the right way to go. I have done this so many times. I remember during my sophomore year of college, it became increasingly clear that I would not be able to afford to return to school for my junior year. It all felt strange. God had directed me to this school in Michigan, but now it seemed He was leading me elsewhere. My parents encouraged me to apply to state schools in North Carolina where they lived so that I could finish my education. I applied and began to tell people at my college that I was leaving because my family could not afford for me to continue. Two families caught wind of this and went to the school to protest that, as a missionary kid, I should be able to stay. They began working on a missionary kid scholarship. I remember scouring the pages of Scripture for some assurance of the direction of my life. The summer before my junior year, I still did not know where I would be going in the fall.

I did not know if the missionary kid scholarship would be ready or if I would be off to the state school. I remember pleading with God for direction, but I never got a clear answer. Instead, I was continually prompted to trust Him with my future. Right before school started, I got the phone call. "You can return to college this year. You got the scholarship!" Happy tears streamed down my face. I'd had to trust that no matter the direction, God was going to be with me in it.

The book of Proverbs shows us that the Bible is not as much about the right way (just life direction or signposts telling us what to do) as about the righteous way: "The path of the righteous is like the morning sun, shining ever brighter till the full light of day" (Proverbs 4:18). The Bible shows us much more than just which direction to go: it teaches us how to grow in holiness and trust the Lord while we wait. The Holy Spirit changes us through Scripture. The truth is this: a foundational belief in Christianity involves trusting that God is guiding us through the power of His Spirit, even if the Bible doesn't always provide specific guidelines for our choices.

The Spirit will direct us in the way we should go, but this guidance will always be in line with God's Word, and it will take us down paths of righteousness. There are times the Spirit is clear in direction and other times we are called to trust Him with our next steps. Truth in the Bible is revealed by the power of the Spirit if, as we read, we are saying yes to discovering God's plan for humanity, not merely looking for a detailed step-by-step guide for ourselves. God guides us through His Word in more than just wisdom for decision-making. He also guides us in how to live. I love how Randy Alcorn puts it: "The distance between me and God's revelation is the distance between me and my Bible. I should prayerfully ask for the Holy Spirit's guidance in my biblical study, but not ask Him for new revelation independent of it."[1]

The truth is, we walk hand in hand with God and learn to trust His leading in and through the pages of Scripture. We cannot ignore the Spirit's work in Bible study. He helps us understand what we're reading. We also know the Spirit guides us into truth (see John 16:13). He teaches us and helps us interpret Scripture (see John 14:26; 1 Corinthians 2:13). He does this by making the text come alive to us. When we become believers, we can be confident that the Spirit is already leading us and directing our lives. As we read the Bible, we may feel nudged to change and grow so we become more like Christ. The Spirit transforms us through the pages of Scripture. I remember one instance when I felt discouraged about my calling to ministry. I had recently seen a woman teach, and she was phenomenal. The comparison trap began to eat away at me. That day as I opened my Bible, I read,

His pleasure is not in the strength of the horse,
    nor his delight in the legs of the warrior;
the LORD delights in those who fear him,
    who put their hope in his unfailing love.
PSALM 147:10-11, NIV

This passage reminded me that God delights in our hearts, not our human strength or charisma. He delights in those who put Him first and desire to please Him. The Spirit has been faithful to guide me in and through the pages of Scripture through every small and large issue in my life. Every time I have prayed and brought things before Him, He has been faithful to answer in His way and His time. It might not always be the way I wish it was, but when the answer is made clear, it has come in and through the pages of Scripture. When we spend time in the Word, we are often pleasantly surprised by how the Lord speaks to our hearts.

I have been asked this question before: "Why do we need to

learn to study the Scriptures when we have the Holy Spirit to guide us?" Again, I love what Randy Alcorn says on this topic: "While the Holy Spirit's presence in the life of the reader is necessary for total biblical understanding, it is not sufficient for it. The Holy Spirit is not a 'cure-all' for poor interpretation. He does not automatically reverse the consequences of violating hermeneutical principles."[2] Alcorn is basically saying that we can't just assume the Holy Spirit will fill in the gaps when we interpret the Bible incorrectly. The Spirit is key to our understanding of Scripture, but we still need to study and read it to the best of our ability. We still need to learn the principles that guide our reading of God's Word. The Holy Spirit's presence is a wonderful guide to our Bible study, but it is also important we be good stewards of learning about the Bible because it is the most important book in our lives. As I mentioned earlier, regardless of where you are in your Bible study—whether a beginner or advanced in your journey—the Spirit will speak to you through His Word. It is just so joyful to deepen your knowledge of the Bible. I think you will be surprised by how exciting it is to really understand how to interpret the text.

As R. C. Sproul puts it in his book *Knowing Scripture*, when it comes to literary principles and hermeneutics, we need to adhere to the rules of interpretation when we come to the Bible—just as we would for any other book.

For the spiritual benefit of applying the words of Scripture to our lives, prayer is enormously helpful. To illumine the spiritual significance of a text, the Holy Spirit is quite important. . . . But to discern the difference between historical narrative and metaphor, prayer is not a great help—unless it involves earnest supplication to God to give us clear minds and pure hearts to overcome our prejudices. Sanctification of the heart is vital for our minds to be free to hear what the Word is saying. We should also pray that God will assist us to overcome our proclivity for slothfulness and make us diligent students of Scripture.[3]

Inspired, Inerrant, Infallible

I first heard about John Howland when I attended an event with my husband. I stirred in my chair as we listened to a speaker tell the story of Howland. It was the first I had ever heard of him. Howland was one of the Pilgrims aboard the *Mayflower* in 1620. He was a servant on the ship, and his story is one of epic proportions. One day, a storm threatened to capsize the *Mayflower*. Many people below deck were vomiting, so Howland climbed to the upper deck to get some air. Due to the extraordinarily rough and tumultuous winds and waves, he fell overboard. But that was not the end of John Howland! By a miraculous turn of events, he managed to grab onto a rope. Before he knew it, the crew caught him with a boat hook and hoisted him back onto the deck.

As one book describes it, the very "hand of God . . . reached out and saved him."[4] Howland held on to the rope, but it was God's sovereign design that drew him back onto the boat.

John Howland had to grab the rope and the crew had to haul him aboard, but God was the One who made it possible. Similarly, the human writers of the Bible put the words on the page, but God was the One who gave them the message. The big, theological words we use to describe the Bible include *inspired*, *inerrant*, and *infallible*. Paul describes God's Word this way: "All Scripture is God-breathed and is useful for teaching, rebuking, correcting and training in righteousness" (2 Timothy 3:16). This doctrine is known as the inspiration of the Bible. The Bible says precisely what God intended it to say. The human authors—all with different writing styles, personalities, experiences, and education levels—served as vessels through which God's authoritative Word was penned. God moved the human authors to write, but there is only one divine Author of the Bible: God Himself.

Inerrancy means we believe the Bible is without error. The Word of God is trustworthy. We can rely on it because it is perfect—after all, God wrote it. In John 17:17, Jesus prays for His people: "Make them holy by your truth; teach them your word, which is truth" (NLT).

Lastly, the Bible is infallible. It is our divine authority for life and godliness. The entirety of the Bible is wholly true. Some people use the words *infallible* and *inerrant* interchangeably and the differences, if any, are slight, but *infallible* means not capable of any error, and *inerrant* means without error.[5]

When we understand how God sovereignly guides and directs, we realize that the Bible is a letter of grace. Grace because it leads us toward truth in a world full of lies. The Bible reveals who God is in a world of stormy chaos and serves as an anchor that we can rely on in tumultuous waters that threaten to sweep us away. Picture John Howland's feet becoming steady on the ship's deck. The Bible is a lifeline to those experiencing the chaos of this world. It can give us firm footing no matter what we're facing.

The author Luke wrote 27.5 percent of the New Testament, making him the largest contributing writer to the New Testament.[6] At the beginning of the book of Luke, he says that he wrote an orderly account "so that you may know the certainty of the things you have been taught" (Luke 1:4). The Bible gives us certainty and assurance about our lives. It is reliable and without error. What the Bible foretells will come to pass, and what it says about the past did happen.

> *The Bible is a lifeline to those experiencing the chaos of this world.*

In many translations, *amen* is the last word in the Bible (see Revelation 22:21). The meaning of *amen*, a Hebrew word, is "truly." It also means "that's truth."[7] Sometimes it is used to express agreement or the sense of "So be it." When we understand the certainty of Scripture, we agree in our minds and hearts with what it says. We can also proclaim, "So be it." We can let the truths of God's Kingdom settle in our hearts and minds—and guide how we see the world. In the words of R. C. Sproul, "Therefore, the expression 'amen' is not simply an acknowledgment of personal agreement with what has been stated; it is an expression of willingness to submit to the implications of that word, to indeed be bound by it, as if the Word of God would put ropes around us not to strangle or retard us but to hold us firmly in place."[8] Reading the Bible is not just about comprehending its words. It is about obeying its message.

First Impressions

My ninth-grade year, we returned to America to visit supporters and raise money—and so my mom could work on her master's in New Testament studies at Gordon-Conwell Theological Seminary. We left Thailand for a year and moved to Needham, Massachusetts, the day before school started. To say it was culture shock would be an understatement. This was before Airbnb, so we ended up moving into the house of an older couple who were traveling that year and generously loaned their home to us. It was within driving distance of my mom's school, so living there made sense. I set my Bible on the bedside table covered with lace doilies, put my new-to-me heels on the shoe rack, and said good night to the floral wallpaper. The day after moving in, I saw the town I would live in that year as I passed through on the way to my first day of school. A Starbucks downtown, rows of fancy houses, and a *huge* American high school. I remember the day so vividly because it was all so overwhelming—new town, new school, new country.

I remember going to youth group one of our first weeks in Massachusetts. I ran to the bathroom, dabbing my underarms with toilet paper and thinking, *Who knew you could sweat in the winter?* I was so nervous because I had no idea what to expect— plus the heat was turned up so high! My armpits were soaking wet, creating pit stains on my sweater. Finding a Christian here in New England had felt like trying to swat and kill a pesky house- fly, near impossible. Yet here at my youth group in the town of Natick, Massachusetts, sat two Christians: a nerdy-looking boy and a beautiful girl with all the right clothes and makeup. I remember wondering how I could impress the popular girl. I looked down at my missionary kid attire. I had picked out my whole outfit for free from a missionary donation bin. At that moment, on that cold Massachusetts night, I realized that the purple van that dropped me off at youth group, the old lady pumps I thought might be "artsy," and the secondhand treasures I was wearing communicated truths about me that I did not want to communicate. You can probably imagine the first impression I made on the people of Natick, Massachusetts.

While I might not have been able to give the impression I desired, God certainly gave us a first impression worth meditat- ing on and understanding thoroughly. He chose to reveal Himself to us through Jesus and the Bible. God's Word is also our first impression of who God is—in other words, the Bible shows us His nature, character, and plan. To live a life pleasing to Him and to build a relationship with Him, we must become familiar with the words in His book.

Revealed through His Word

We learn to love God through the pages of Scripture. We read the Bible to know Him and understand how to live in obedience to Him. There are two terms for the way God reveals Himself: *general revelation* and *special revelation*. General revelation is the idea that God reveals Himself through nature, and all He has created, to all people: "The heavens declare the glory of God, and the sky above proclaims his handiwork" (Psalm 19:1, ESV). His general revelation to all people means everyone can see the incredible world around them, reflect on it, and know that there is a Creator God. No one can say they didn't know (see Romans 1:18-20). When I go hiking or look up at the night sky, I often think of God. I remember Girl Scouts and camping in the mountains of Thailand. Looking up at that starry sky left me breathless, thinking of God and His majestic handiwork. This revelation points us toward God's existence, but it is not sufficient for salvation because we cannot come to fully understand God's plan or character through this type of revelation. We need special revelation to understand God's plan more fully—and to come to a saving faith.

Special revelation is how God reveals Himself through Scripture and His Son, Jesus. When we read and learn about Jesus' time on earth, we understand more about who God is. Since Jesus died, rose again, and ascended to the right hand of God, the special revelation we have now comes through the pages of Scripture. As Psalm 19:7-8 puts it, "The law of the LORD is perfect, reviving the soul; the testimony of the LORD is sure, making wise the simple; the precepts of the LORD are right, rejoicing the heart; the commandment of the LORD is pure, enlightening the eyes" (ESV). There are many differing opinions on how the Spirit communicates with us today—whether God only speaks to us through His Word, or whether the Spirit illuminates God to us by other means as well.

Either way, revelations from the Spirit will never contradict what God has revealed to us through Jesus and Scripture. Other believers may have different thoughts about hearing from the Spirit than we do, but let's remember that *we are called to love each other even with our differences* and to exercise Christian charity.

Recently, I was on the phone with a friend who lamented about a situation with some difficult people in her life. As I listened, I longed to encourage her by reminding her of what God thinks of her circumstances, but no Scripture came to mind. Well, two seconds after we ended the call, I walked into my house, and the subscription service that texts me Bible verses sent this: "The LORD is far from the wicked, but he hears the prayer of the righteous" (Proverbs 15:29). I texted her this verse and was reminded of how powerfully God speaks through His Word. This is one small example of how dynamic the Word of God is—and how timely the Spirit's work in our lives. The Holy Spirit is active, and He uses the Word to continually speak to us.

6

THE ROLE OF PRAYER

EVERY YEAR AT THE COUNTY FAIR my sons want to win a gold-fish. For me, knowing that we have to then go purchase fish food and a bowl means that I try to steer them toward other prizes. But lo and behold, to my dismay, this year we once again came home with two goldfish. If you have ever seen a goldfish in a bowl, you know they cannot hide. You can hold the bowl with two hands and peer inside, and you can see the goldfish no matter where they go. Sometimes when I pray, I picture that goldfish bowl. No matter where I am or what's going on in my life, the Lord sees me and pays attention to me. As the children's song says, "He's got the whole world in His hands, He's got the whole world in His hands." God holds the goldfish bowl, and there is nowhere to hide. This is comforting because He loves us and desires a relationship with us, continually drawing us near and always aware of our everyday struggles. Yet many of us pray as if we are not already known by

God. We pray as if our jealous thoughts, anxious feelings, and anger have somehow passed under the radar of the God of the universe—while we swim around in a crystal-clear bowl. I hate to break it to you, but God can *see* your frustration with that other goldfish. The Word of God "exposes our innermost thoughts and desires" (Hebrews 4:12, NLT), and our prayer life is the vocalization of those innermost desires to a God who already knows them. When we pray, God draws us close in relationship with Him.

When we read the Bible, God holds out His hand, and when we pray, we grasp His hand back. If the Bible is speaking to us, prayer is how we speak back. There is a mutual, intimate partnership between Bible reading and prayer: we are allying with God! Prayer has taken on different forms for me in different seasons. I used to spend long, uninterrupted periods in prayer, but now I have learned to attach certain prayers to everyday habits. For example, I thank God for my children when I zip up their winter coats. Or I might pray for them when I do the dishes. Sometimes, when I'm unable to find the exact words to express what I am feeling through prayer, the Bible gives me the words to say—and that's what it's done for people throughout time.

As I seek to chase sacred in my everyday life, prayer serves several purposes for me. It *communicates* my heart to God, *comforts* me, aligns my concerns with God's, and brings me *clarity*. Prayer is how we communicate with God. It is a way for us to acknowledge that his attention is on everything. It is easy to call our mom and feel seen. In a similar way, prayer is how we surrender our daily frustrations and commitments to a God who sees us. We also get to praise God through prayer and thank Him—expressing our heartfelt gratitude for all He does for us. Prayer also comforts us. Have you ever taken the time to pray for someone who confessed a particular frustration or hardship to you? Prayer reminds them and us that our all-powerful God sympathizes with us and desires to help us. It aligns our concerns with God's by reminding us that we are participants in His Kingdom. We get the privilege of praying about our godly desires, praying when we are concerned about someone or about the state of this world, and more. We get to actively participate in God's plan by praying for His will to be done on earth and in the lives of others. It is a daily reminder of our true citizenship. When we partner with God in prayer and Bible reading, we are chasing His agenda and His Kingdom. We are reminded that we have far more of a purpose than what we can see. Finally, prayer brings clarity. When we pray, we often see and hear more clearly because we are more in tune with our Father in heaven. Clarity comes when we receive a response to the prayers we long to see answered. When our motives are pure and we pray for wisdom, we gain clarity because God gives us that wisdom (see Proverbs 16:2). Prayer helps us remember the One who is sovereign over every situation, and it reminds us that our concerns are His concerns.

Powerful, Honest Prayer

The Bible gives us so many examples of powerful prayer. Just think: Hannah prayed when she was infertile (see 1 Samuel 1:11, 27-28), Paul gave thanks for the church of Ephesus (see Ephesians 1:15-19), and Hezekiah prayed when he was facing imminent attack from the enemy (see Isaiah 37:14-22). The nation of Judah had everything to lose, and Hezekiah turned to God as their ally. We know His will by knowing the Scriptures. And when we pray the Scriptures, we are praying His will.

Prayerfully asking the Lord to reveal Himself through the Bible is a humble posture that surpasses any method of study I can give you. Choosing to come before God in prayerful delight is the key to keeping your understanding of God's communication clear and not garbled. It is crucial to pray before, during, and after your study. One of my favorite practices, which my mom taught me, is to end my prayers with Scripture. This helps us have confidence that God has heard us. One verse we can pray in this way is 1 John 5:14-15: "This is the confidence that we have toward him, that if we ask anything according to his will he hears us. And if we know that he hears us in whatever we ask, we know that we have the requests that we have asked of him" (ESV). Our prayer might go something like this: "Thank You so much, Lord, that this is the confidence we have in approaching You: if we ask anything according to Your will, You hear us!" The promise is not that we will get whatever we want as if God is a genie, but we do know we can be confident that He hears us when we ask.

My little boys love walkie-talkies. They use them to share their plans, communicate back and forth, and enjoy hours and hours of relationship-building. They spread out all through our woods, and I have even seen them use duct tape to attach their walkie-talkies to their bikes and four-wheelers.

"You there?" my son Barkley will say, cupping his hand over the walkie-talkie.

"Yes, it's me!" my son Hudson will respond.

One time, my boys even picked up a random person's voice speaking back! I remember hearing them from downstairs screaming, "Who is this? Who is this?" over their walkie-talkies. They could not get over the fact that walkie-talkies are so fickle that they can pick up another person's communication.

The person answered back, laughing, seeming just as taken aback. "Who is *this*?" The boys finally got so freaked out they ended the conversation. Thankfully, when we open the pages of Scripture, we can rest assured that it is always God who's talking back.

Through prayer, we build an intimate relationship with our Father. In some ways, it's like my sons' walkie-talkie connection. God's walkie-talkie is always charged up. He's always ready to hear from us and take us back, no matter how long it's been since we've prayed. The pages of Scripture are living and active, but we need the power of our prayer life and the Holy Spirit to work through the text on our behalf. We always need to be plugged into our power source. When we approach the text, we must understand that the Spirit is the One who illuminates it for us. A proper application of the text leads to our growth and sanctification.

I have often felt guilty about bringing all my emotions before the Lord. When I feel that way, I'm comforted by the prayers in the Bible. They are *rife* with various feelings and motives, and they're *full* of heartfelt honesty. For goodness' sake, the psalmist felt safe to pray things about his enemies like "May no one extend kindness to him or take pity on his fatherless children" (Psalm 109:12). The psalmist also felt comfortable expressing his deepest grief to God: "Have compassion on me, LORD, for I am weak. Heal me, LORD, for my bones are in agony. I am sick at heart. How long, O LORD, until you restore me?" (Psalm 6:2-3, NLT).

I mean . . . the psalmist let it all out before the Lord. The pages of the Bible model just about every type of prayer: prayers asking for boldness (Acts 4:23-31), prayers of protest and anger (Psalm 10), prayers of repentance (Psalm 51), and prayers asking for consolation or comfort (Psalm 9:7-10). Scripture reminds me that my imperfect prayers put me in good company. Prayer strips us of pretense as our souls are laid bare before the King of kings.

I have become quicker at bringing my envy, sadness, and even my sometimes-competitive spirit before the Lord. Instead of dismissing my emotions or thoughts as silly, I take them to God and ask Him why I feel a certain way. Earlier in my life, I was embarrassed to share with the Lord what I was truly feeling, but I found freedom in the idea that He already knows it all. I ask myself, *What is this emotion teaching me?* And I pray, *Lord, can You help me address this?*

We can be certain that God welcomes our prayers about the state of our circumstances and our hearts. When we pray, we acknowledge that God is powerful and accessible. We pray to a God who has made His will known through His Word.

Approaching an Accessible God

The music pounded as twelve-year-old me looked around. *"Nung, song, sam, see, ha, hook, jet, bat,"* the teacher chanted. My fellow dance students and I were getting ready for our annual performance, and we were all out of sync. We started and restarted again and again. I grew up dancing at a studio in Thailand with primarily Thai students. My favorite class was jazz, which was super high energy and fun. I moved on to enjoy many other dance forms as well, and I just knew I wanted to be a contemporary dancer when I grew up.

Performances were always my favorite part of the class. This particular year, we were preparing to perform on the top story of the mall. I vividly remember the Thai makeup artists applying thick black eyebrow liner over my blonde eyebrows and covering my complexion with the same makeup they used for all the Thai dancers. I look back and laugh at my goofy makeup that did not match my face. We waited and waited and waited. Our performance ended up being delayed for hours because the princess of Thailand was coming to watch, and her flight had gotten delayed. In Thailand, royalty is highly respected, so the show did not go on until she arrived.

At the end of the performance, it was customary to pay respect to Her Highness. When you approach a member of the Thai royal family, you must crawl on your hands and knees. The entire dance class had to crawl into her presence. We had to bow our heads and look downward because looking up would have been considered disrespectful. We were not even allowed to be too close to her because her status was so much greater than ours. There are many rules and regulations regarding royalty in Thailand, especially concerning the king. For example, you can't use your foot to stop a coin from rolling away because your foot—the most unclean part of your body—would touch the image of his head on the coin. Throughout the city, the king's birthday is honored with massive celebrations, and every soup shop and restaurant has the king and queen's picture hanging up! When I was a kid, before every movie we had to stand for the king's national anthem as we watched him cross the screen. We would see footage of him giving to the poor, helping the elderly, and walking as people waved the Thai flag at him. To honor and love the king was a way of life.

Scripture tells us we have direct access to the King of kings, and our King welcomes us. The Bible says that we can approach Him with anything at any time, and we can come to Christ confident that He hears us. The barrier of sin between us and God has been eliminated because of Jesus' death on the cross. In spite of this amazing gift, many of us remain prayerless as if something stops us from approaching Christ in complete confidence. I love how Hebrews 4:16 says it: "So let us come boldly to the throne of our gracious God. There we will receive his mercy, and we will find grace to help us when we need it most" (NLT).

Ephesians also tells us that we have direct access to the King of the universe: "Because of Christ and our faith in him, we can now come boldly and confidently into God's presence" (Ephesians 3:12, NLT). We can come to God through prayer and Scripture reading because of Jesus and our belief in Him! When we pray, we are not just bystanders but active participants in God's plan. Praying and placing ourselves in proximity to His Word are intentional pursuits of a relationship with Christ.

We Need Humility

We need humility to value prayer. Just as a lack of Bible reading can be due to overconfidence in our ability to do life on our own, or a lack of in-depth Bible study can be due to believing we already know how to study the Bible, a lack of prayer can also be due to feeling like we already know or have what we need. Paul E. Miller explains it like this in his book *A Praying Life*: "If you are not praying, then you are quietly confident that time, money, and talent are all you need in life. You'll always be a little too tired, a little too busy. But if, like Jesus, you realize you can't do life on your own, then no matter how busy, no matter how tired you are, you will find the time to pray."[1]

So what is stopping us from praying? Why do most of us remain stuck, not participating in prayer? There are so many reasons people do not pray—and maybe, like me, you have struggled with feeling like you aren't even *good* at praying. You know how when someone prays out loud, you think, *Wow, they are good at praying!*? But God never asked us to be good at praying. No, He actually says, "And when you pray, do not be like the hypocrites, for they love to pray standing in the synagogues and on the street corners to be seen by others. Truly I tell you, they have received their reward in full" (Matthew 6:5). God actually desires that we have a humble heart in prayer. I don't know about you, but because I feel like I am not *good* at praying, I'm more reliant on God when I am asked to pray out loud.

Do you remember how I wrote earlier about the time my future husband and I broke up? At that time, I found it hard to pray. I thought God had directly led me to this man! I felt abandoned by him, and in turn I felt abandoned by God. I did not have an accurate view of God in this season. I did not believe God was good, so I did not think things were happening *for* my good. Even though

I did not want to, I continued to open up my Bible. I told God I did not feel like it and did not want to pray! He was so gracious to me during that season, and I learned so much by being honest with Him.

In the gospels, we see that Jesus' motivation for praying wasn't about looking good. He prayed out of His great need for His Father. Our awareness of our need is directly related to our prayer life. When we acknowledge how much we need God, our prayer life is greatly improved, but when we are prideful and think we can do everything ourselves, our prayer life is weakened.

Because I feel like I am not good at praying, I'm more reliant on God when I am asked to pray.

Prayer as Preparation

I am struck by Jesus' last prayers before going to the cross. He tells His disciples to "watch and pray so that you will not fall into temptation. The spirit is willing, but the flesh is weak" (Matthew 26:41). The disciples demonstrate the truth of Jesus' point by *falling asleep* in Jesus' great hour of need—their flesh was weak! In the Gospel of Luke, this same story is recorded, but Jesus instructs them twice to pray so "that you will not fall into temptation" (Luke 22:40, 46).

Earlier in Matthew, when teaching the disciples to pray, Jesus models what we know as the Lord's Prayer: "And lead us not into temptation, but deliver us from evil" (6:13, ESV). Prayer reminds us that we are sinners and will be tempted to do evil. In wisdom, we pray not only against temptation when we come up against it, but we also pray beforehand, in preparation. If we have a spirit of humility, we will acknowledge, *I might sin. I might be tempted because my flesh is weak, so I must pray to ask the Lord for strength.* However, if we have a spirit of pride, we will be unprepared to face temptation because we think we have what we need already.

I also often feel this in the way I pray for my kids. Instead of praying *for* my kids using the Scriptures, I tend to react to my kids' behavior by praying *against* what I see. But in recent years I have worked to pray proactively as well as reactively. Of course God honors both kinds of prayer, but I want to ask God to prepare them for the challenges and temptations they will face. One way I pray proactively for my kids starts when they are still in the womb. Before they're born, I ask the Lord for a life verse to pray over them. I then pray that life verse for them every single night before bed. May they conform to His Word through the prayers of a tired, desperate mama. I picked these verses for my children before the trials, temptations, and hard times could come. In case you're wondering, here are the verses I've chosen for each of my kids:

In wisdom, we pray not only against temptation when we come up against it, but we also pray beforehand, in preparation.

Paxton:

> We are his workmanship, created in Christ Jesus for good works, which God prepared beforehand, that we should walk in them.
>
> EPHESIANS 2:10, ESV

Barkley:

> Get rid of all bitterness, rage and anger, brawling and slander, along with every form of malice. Be kind and compassionate to one another, forgiving each other, just as in Christ God forgave you.
>
> EPHESIANS 4:31-32

Hudson:

> He has shown you, O mortal, what is good.
>   And what does the LORD require of you?
> To act justly and to love mercy
>   and to walk humbly with your God.
>
> MICAH 6:8

Copley:

> The fear of the LORD is the beginning of wisdom,
>   and knowledge of the Holy One is understanding.
>
> PROVERBS 9:10

Tatum:

> Before I formed you in the womb I knew you,
>   before you were born I set you apart;
>   I appointed you as a prophet to the nations.
>
> JEREMIAH 1:5

Choosing life verses for your kids is a beautiful way to pray for them to align with God's Word in their speech, deeds, and entire lives. I would encourage anyone and everyone to do this and see how God answers those prayers. If you want to participate in this type of prayer, I suggest beginning by asking the Lord to reveal a good life verse for your child. As you read the Word of God, He will make it clear which is the perfect verse for them! That is how I went about choosing life verses for my kids.

According to a commentary on the book of James, "Since God's Word is the means of regeneration (James 1:18), a right response to the Word is appropriately presented as the initial test of a vital faith. For the believer to accept regeneration through the

Word is one thing; to permit the Word to work spiritual maturity in him is another."[2]

Furthermore, humility is an attribute that's necessary to further our prayer lives. Prayer is the source of our strength; when we need the power to fuel our days, we pray. So where does Jesus return to in His most difficult trials? To prayer and the Word. Jesus spent His last moments on earth not teaching, performing miracles, or participating in community outreach—but praying the Word of God. On the cross, He cried out the words of Psalm 22:1: "My God, my God, why have you forsaken me?" (Matthew 27:46). His last words on the cross were a prayer from Psalm 31:5: "Father, into your hands I commit my spirit" (Luke 23:46).

Jesus quotes Scripture in His sorrows. He quotes Scripture in His fears. He speaks to God in the language of Scripture. Not only does this show that the Word of God is fulfilled in Jesus, but it also shows us that all the prophecies of the Old Testament point to Him. When He speaks these words, He declares that He is the one we can trust. Other people will mislead us, forsake us, and misunderstand us, but Christ never will. In the face of our insufficiency, we find the leaning life: a life of dependency on Him.

Prayer as a Path to Peace

Every single night, my son Hudson asks me how I position myself to fall asleep. I adjust his pillow and position him by putting his right arm under the pillow. "I fall asleep holding my pillow, bud. I lay on my side." As I say this, I gently shift his body and position him like I typically fall asleep at night.

He reminds me again, "I want to sleep like you, Mom. I want to sleep just like you!"

So, every night like clockwork, I take his little hand and slip it under the pillow, and his hand grasps the pillow tightly as he turns his cheek to rest his head on the pillowcase. "Like this, bud. Just like this," I say quietly.

Like my son, all of us are looking for a cushion of control that will keep us calm. A buffer that we can hold, a pillow that can help us sleep at night or calm our anxious hearts. When our lives feel chaotic or out of our control, we try to find something we can grasp tightly. Usually, this is something we can do on our own, or sometimes we compare ourselves to others and try to do whatever other people find peace in. We might look like we have control of our lives if we enjoy fulfilling relationships, go on those vacations, parent our kids in an orderly way, or have a successful career. But time and time again, our self-sufficiencies will fail us. When everything is in upheaval and your life feels upside down, where do you run?

Control or order becomes an idol when Christ is not the control center, when the Word of God is not our baseline of order. When our lives have a measure of control or order, we find we can sleep. We can breathe and our lives feel fulfilling, but when our axles come undone and suffering comes knocking, we begin to grasp at our pillows, hoping they will stabilize us. Christ must be our cushion. We must be able to submit our chaos to His control and ask Him to calm our racing thoughts at night and during the day. He must be the one we process with, the one we pray to, and the one we turn to before temptation comes. When we chase sacred, our goal is to live from a place where Jesus is our peace, where we know we are loved. We won't be striving or searching for that which will complete us—we will already be complete and able to move forward from a posture of prayer and a groundedness in His Word.

When my husband and I went to Vegas on vacation, we brought our son Barkley, who was one at the time. We hired a babysitter so we could have some time to ourselves. My husband and I left for dinner one night and returned later to our beloved

Barkley, asleep in his crib. But there was also an inanimate object in the crib with him. The lights were low, and the babysitter was still awake. I looked over at her. "What is he holding?" I asked.

She laughed. "He is holding a bagel. He would not let it go. So I just put him to sleep holding it."

I gasped. *He is sleeping with a bagel in his arms?* I couldn't stop laughing. What a sight. I pried the bagel out of his tight grip, and he continued to sleep soundly.

When God takes our bagels—our means of self-preservation— we may feel that our lives are going to crumble into chaos. But our efforts to protect and provide for ourselves only give us false security. No matter what number is in our bank account or how many followers we have, one day these things will let us down. Where we turn for security will directly influence who we become. Will we turn to God through His Word and prayer, or will we rely on the promises of the world around us?

When we are unable or unequipped to take the next step, we can pray. I love how 1 Peter 5:7 puts it: "Cast all your anxiety on him because he cares for you." I also love this translation of Philippians 4:6-7: "Don't worry about anything, but in all your prayers ask God for what you need, always asking him with a thankful heart. And God's peace, which is far beyond human understanding, will keep your hearts and minds safe in union with Christ Jesus" (GNT).

Prayer is the sensible response to having access to our loving King. The more we pray, the more we acknowledge our need for God. It is the perfect response to hearing from God in His Word. When we worry, Scripture tells us to pray. Prayer is the only thing that can truly restore our peace in the middle of a chaotic, restless world.

PART 3

How Do We Chase Sacred?

7

WHICH BIBLE
SHOULD YOU CHOOSE?

ONE OF THE FIRST THINGS I noticed when I moved to America for a year at the age of fifteen was the grocery stores. Walk down the aisles of an American grocery store and you'll see rows and rows of cereal boxes, each to fit your fancy. The endless choices are overwhelming. Choices are something we take for granted day in and day out in America—we do this without even knowing it. We are also prone to taking our access to the Bible in English for granted. Growing up in Western culture, choosing a Bible is equivalent to walking along the endless grocery store rows and selecting the exact cereal you prefer. Would you like it made of wheat or oats? Or maybe you want it sugary and geared toward kids? Do you want a study Bible? A personal application Bible? A teen study Bible?

Comparatively, imagine what it would be like to have just *one* partially finished translation in your language. This is the reality for many believers around the world. Halfway across the globe, there is a tiny village with faithful believers who attend church multiple times a week. The pastor preaches in the native language but reads and explains the Bible in a different language. If you want to read the Bible, you need to attend Sunday school to learn *that* language. In 2010, the New Testament was completed for this minority language. The children were taught how to read and write their own language, but most of the older people never had that opportunity. A faithful Christian woman of eighty-six years old was so interested in reading the Bible in her very own language that she learned how to read—after a lifetime of trying to understand God's Word in a different language. I want to impress upon you that if an eighty-six-year-old lady could teach herself how to read because she wanted so badly to access God's Word, we can thank God for our access to Scripture in so many excellent English translations.

How Do I Decide?

Funnily enough, there is much confusion and chaos surrounding Bible translations. "Which translation should I use? Why do some people claim only one translation is a viable option?" Maybe you have asked one of these questions or experienced confusion about which translation is best. I know that doing online ministry, I get questions like these often.

Some of my earliest memories of growing up in Thailand involve weaving in and out of traffic on a motorbike. Westerners might think there is a lack of structure or rules when they experience driving there. Thailand has rules, but some of the rules are different from those in the United States. And sometimes there is an unspoken understanding that those road rules do not matter—and that speed limits and helmets are mere suggestions. The marketplace was one of my favorite destinations: the yelling vendors, the mismatch of different types of food, and the swatting at flies that landed strategically on the meat. But one of my all-time favorite places to shop was the night bazaar, which I mentioned earlier in the book when I referred to the pirated movies. I would listen in on tourists haphazardly trying to communicate in English. In response, the shop owners used broken words to explain the price, model, and product. The language barrier was immense, and I often giggled at the miscommunications.

Sometimes picking a translation can feel that way: "Am I getting the real deal? Is this translation an accurate representation of God's Word? What about the language barrier?" Yet the stakes are much higher for God's Word than for a cheap knockoff purse. The first truth that I am happy to report is this: the scholarship of our English translations is trustworthy, and there are so many reasons to be thankful for them.

Seeing these differences increases our understanding of God's Word, especially when we approach it with humility and a curious heart.

The first tip I would give you in picking a Bible translation is this: try several and compare them. Bounce around before you settle on one. There are many excellent English translations, and the scholars have worked tirelessly to translate the text. Americans have common usage translations, such as the New International Version (NIV), and we also have lesser known ones, such as the New English Translation (NET). There is such a variety of translations, including the New Living Translation (NLT), the English Standard Version (ESV), and the Christian Standard Bible (CSB).

I love to compare different translations because they vary in style and how they interpret particular sentences from Hebrew or Greek. When we compare translations, we will notice passages where scholars have different translation philosophies. Seeing these differences increases our understanding of God's Word, especially when we approach it with humility and a curious heart.

Translation Philosophies

Every translation you read has its own philosophy regarding the culture in which the text was written, the language, and grammar. Bible translators often talk about two main philosophies: word-for-word literal translations (formal equivalence) and thought-for-thought translations (dynamic equivalence). Both consider wording, sentence structure, and readability, but they have several key differences.

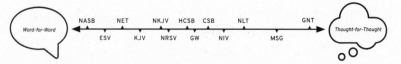

A literal word-for-word translation looks at each word instead of the general meaning of an entire passage. Scholars using this approach translate the words precisely and then make sure they all work together. They try to stay as close as possible to the original meaning of each Greek or Hebrew word, while still seeking to represent English sentence structure. The downside is that this approach will often result in clunkier syntax.

A thought-for-thought translation focuses on the intended purpose of the passage first while still trying to stay as close to the original wording as possible. One of the benefits of a dynamic translation is its readability. It concentrates on making sure the overall meaning in the Greek or Hebrew is represented in another language clearly and naturally. This approach might need to change the sentence form, yet it also tries to remain true and accurate to the meaning of the words in the original.

Before you choose one or the other, I recommend comparing translations in both categories. If you are looking for a readable and accurate translation but don't want to spend the time comparing several, I recommend staying in the middle, choosing a translation (such as the NIV) that includes elements of both dynamic and formal equivalence. Yet if you are recommending a Bible to a new believer, a dynamic equivalence translation (like the NLT) would be the best recommendation. These versions make the text easier to understand in English and more accessible for a new believer to read.

My mom told me a story from when we were young and living in the US. We invited some neighborhood kids to a church program. These neighbors were not believers, and they had never experienced church before. We piled into the car and, once at church, spent the evening playing games and listening to Bible stories. At the end of the evening, we were given a colorful handout encouraging us to memorize a Bible verse. The verse was in a version that was more formally equivalent. It reflected the form and structure of the Greek text, though it was written in English. On the way home, my mom asked the neighbor boy how he enjoyed his time. He responded by saying that he had a wonderful time, especially during the games. Then he held up the handout and said, "But I don't understand these poems that we were given!" This is an excellent example of an accurate translation that doesn't communicate clearly to its audience.

No translation is completely literal, not even those that value formal equivalence. Often I overhear people saying that they want the most literal translation, or they ask, "What is a good literal translation?" Many people value a literal Bible. When you translate one language into another, it is technically impossible to do so literally while preserving the meaning. Here is an example to show you what a verse would look like if it were actually translated word for word, exchanging English for Greek. First, I'll give an exact word-for-word gloss of 1 Corinthians 4:4 in the original Greek. I'll shift to a formal equivalence translation and then slowly move toward a more dynamic equivalence translation.

οὐδὲν γὰρ ἐμαυτῷ σύνοιδα, ἀλλ' οὐκ ἐν τούτῳ δεδικαίωμαι, ὁ δὲ ἀνακρίνων με Κύριός ἐστιν.

[of] nothing for against-myself I-am-aware, but not in this I-have-been-justified, the but one-examining me Lord is (word-for-word of Greek)

I am not aware of anything against myself, but I am not thereby acquitted. It is the Lord who judges me. (New Revised Standard Version 1989: formal equivalence)

My conscience is clear, but that does not make me innocent. It is the Lord who judges me. (New International Version 2011: in the middle between formal and dynamic)

My conscience is clear, but that doesn't prove I'm right. It is the Lord himself who will examine me and decide. (New Living Translation 2004: dynamic equivalence)

My conscience is clear, but that does not prove that I am really innocent. The Lord is the one who passes judgment on me. (Good News Translation 1992: dynamic equivalence)

Let's reflect. What differences do you notice? Are some verse translations easier for you to understand than others? Do you think they each mean the same thing?

Considering the Receptor Language

Languages are very complex, so when we think about translation work, we must consider how many unique aspects there are to every language. Each translation tries to stay close to the Greek and Hebrew text while taking into account the receptor language (the language that the Bible is being translated into). For most of you reading this book, your receptor language is English. Every translator deals with a receptor culture. In the example of 1 Corinthians 4:4 above, you can see some of the translators felt that the phrase "my conscience is clear" is the best representation of what an English speaker might actually say (as opposed to the literal Greek: "[of] nothing for against-myself I-am-aware").

For another example, in Southeast Asia, where my parents translate the Bible, people eat snakes. So, when dealing with Matthew 7:9-11, the translation team had to make some choices based on the culture and the original intent of the passage. Matthew 7:9-11 says, "Which of you, if your son asks for bread, will give him a stone? Or if he asks for a fish, will give him a snake? If you, then, though you are evil, know how to give good gifts to your children, how much more will your Father in heaven give good gifts to those who ask him!"

For a first-century Jew reading this passage, it would have been against Jewish dietary laws to eat a snake. Snakes were considered unclean and were forbidden as a food choice. So the original reader might ask, "What type of father would force their child to do something forbidden by the law?" As Americans, we look at this passage and think, *Of course I would not give my child a snake,* because we believe snakes are scary, dangerous, and gross. We have the intended emotional response when we read the verse even though we do not understand how a first-century Jew would respond to that suggestion. But the people of this Southeast Asian language eat snakes and would not see a problem with giving one to their son. If they read the verse, they would think to themselves, *Of course I would give my son a snake if I didn't have a fish!* The actual meaning of the passage would be completely lost. One of the ways a translator could deal with this would be to specify a type of snake that the people group would not eat, such as a cobra. Then the translator could explain in the footnotes that the Jews would not give their son a snake of any kind.

I will give you a few further examples of the kinds of choices translators have to make when considering the receptor language and the ancient languages of the Bible. Let's look at this verse from James: "My dear brothers and sisters, take note of this: Everyone should be quick to listen, slow to speak and slow to become angry" (1:19). After a national translator (a local trained to translate the Bible into their own language) has worked very hard on their translation, it will go through rigorous checking and testing to ensure it is clear, accurate, and natural. In this case, someone asked the national translator to give an example of what "be slow to speak" means in his culture and language. The translator replied, "It means to taaaallllkkkkkkkkk . . . liiiiiiiiiiiiiike . . . thiiiiisssssssss." Picture for yourself an entire congregation speaking very slowly to each other because James told them to! Well, that is not the intended meaning, so the translators needed to use the wording "think before you speak" so that the meaning was not lost.

Before Jesus' death on the cross, He went to pray in the garden of Gethsemane. Guards arrested Him. Although moments earlier the disciples had failed to pray and fallen asleep, now Peter decided to defend Christ. Peter cut off the ear of the high priest's servant, and then Jesus responded, "Enough of this!" He touched the man's ear and healed him (see Luke 22:50-51, GNT). In this example, the English word *enough* translated into the Southeast Asian language would mean *perfect*, so Jesus' words would read, "Perfect! That's perfect!" which could be taken to mean "Great job cutting off the ear!" That meaning would not work, so the translation had to change. Translators are always asking the question "What is the intended meaning of the passage?" They are also asking, "Is the intended meaning being communicated clearly in this culture and this language?" We, as Bible students, should be asking this same question when we approach our Bibles.

Gratitude and Joy

The history of the creation of your English Bible is littered with persecution of translators. The translation you hold in your hand today came with sacrifice: harassment, persecution, and even martyrdom. John Wycliffe (one of the most famous Bible translators), who translated the Bible from Latin into English in the fourteenth century, earned the name "heretic" for believing that all people, not just the elite and educated, should be able to read their Bible in a language they could understand. After he died, his opponents crushed his bones and lit them on fire. Another famous Bible translator, William Tyndale, smuggled Bibles into England in the sixteenth century and was strangled before being burned at the stake for completing his translation of the New Testament.

Today, many Bible translators worldwide still experience lots of spiritual warfare. Satan does not want you to read your Bible. When my parents finished translating the New Testament, our family and the national translator faced numerous challenges, incredible opposition, and spiritual warfare. As I mentioned earlier, our house flooded two times the year my parents finished the New Testament. I remember bailing water late into the night, scooping and throwing it out the window. My mom, who knew how to get us kids riled up, joked about the fact that she had "just fertilized the lawn with manure," because everything previously on that lawn was now flowing inside. We were too old and cynical to find it funny that our clothes were soiled in poop. (I was fifteen at the time.) But that wasn't all. Shortly before the floods, my mom, brother, and I had been hospitalized with dengue fever. My mom had a tough time recovering. Our bones ached, and the pain was severe. I had nurses pricking my finger by the end of the week. They seemed to think it was hilarious to watch a girl afraid of needles scream at the top of her lungs from a tiny prick on the finger. I remember this time as the beginning of the onset of my depression. One of the effects of dengue fever is depression for months or years afterward. Years down the line, I can look back and see the correlation, but back then, it was hard to understand why I suddenly struggled daily with my mental health. I could go on. That year was so difficult for our family for many reasons, but our dear friend and national translator suffered even more. While he was out of the country, his father died; his brother died and left behind several children who needed his support; his crops were ruined; and his health suffered. We often don't reflect on the truth that good things come from suffering. Jesus gives us the ultimate example of this in His death on the cross for us, by which He provided us with new life and salvation. In giving these examples of opposition faced by Bible translators, I long for you to have a great appreciation for reading the Bible in a language that is your own, no matter which translation you choose.

When my parents came back to America one year to visit family and friends and to share with churches about Bible translation, they knew that one of the churches was in the middle of a debate about which Bible translation to use. The pastor and one of the elders shared a very strong opinion and advocated for a certain English translation, communicating that all others were inaccurate. They wanted to spend the money to eliminate all the Bibles in the pews and replace them with this one translation. My parents were sitting in a service at that church when the pastor asked everyone to open their Bibles. They noticed that the lady in front of them didn't have a Bible with her, and

No matter which translation of the Bible you choose, I hope that you approach it with confidence and enthusiasm.

there must not have been one in front of her in the pew, so she reached behind her for the Bible in front of my parents. Seeing that it was a different translation from the one the pastor and elder were promoting, she cringed a bit and replaced the Bible in the pew, having chosen not to use it. It broke my parents' hearts to see that this kind of confusion was hindering people and giving them a great amount of insecurity about the Word.

No matter which translation of the Bible you choose, I hope that you approach it with confidence and enthusiasm. We should be able to rejoice in the fact that we have so many English translations available when so many people worldwide don't even have one, or they have only the New Testament. An orderly approach to your study of the Word should include humbly, inquisitively comparing several translations with gratitude and joy.

IV.

OBSERVE AND ASK

ONE DAY MANY YEARS AGO, my now-husband, Jamie, randomly walked into a local pizza joint in his small town. This pizza joint and sub shop is one of the only restaurants we have in the town that we now live in. I love to joke that every love worth having starts at Pizza Haven. Jamie was covered in concrete dust that day, but under the dust I could see the brightest blue eyes. He had recently started a concrete foundation company and had stopped the pace of his grueling day to get a grilled chicken sub. He was single and wishing he could meet the love of his life and settle down, but things had not worked out that way for him. He had watched all his peers get married and have kid after kid as he continued to travel, work, and wish he could start a family of his own.

Meanwhile a peppy, blonde college girl home for break was eating lunch in the same pizza place with Jamie's littlest sister.

You guessed it—that college girl was me! My parents were back in Thailand, so during my breaks in college I went to my grandparents' house in New Hampshire. My dad had grown up nearby, which meant that I had met Jamie's sister when we came to America one year to live with my grandparents and raise support. The church Jamie grew up in actually supported us as missionaries. Jamie is ten years my senior, so even though his sister and I had been pen pals growing up since meeting each other at the age of four—her writing from America, me writing from Thailand—I didn't have any memories that involved him.

His first words to me were "Wow, you grew up!" (Later he said he remembered me from when my family visited the church in New Hampshire that supported us.)

My thoughts: *Uh-huhhh?*

Now, to keep things short and sweet, my husband was born and raised a "New Hampshaaaa" boy and would die on his New Hampshire pride. I, on the other hand, was a third-culture kid struggling to make sense of where I fit. After some years of dating Jamie, I agreed to marry him, under one condition: "We *will not* stay or live in New Hampshire." I had been in the town often enough over the years to know that I would never be able to fit in due to the lack of diversity and Asian food. I had grown up surrounded by many different cultures, and there seemed to be no culture in the little town he lived in. Well, God had other things in mind, and we are still living in this town. But now I can say God really knew what he was doing.

Jamie and I made our promises, exchanged vows, and were married. I spent the next two years in New York City pursuing my dreams of becoming a professional dancer while he built up his business in New Hampshire. We lived apart for those first years of marriage, and I remember thinking it was wedded bliss. Seeing each other on the weekends was way too much fun! After those first couple years, we got pregnant. And as we discussed the future, it became clear to me that my husband had no intention of leaving his hometown. He had built a successful business here and, to my dismay, starting over did not make financial sense for us. All his contacts for building were in New Hampshire. If he wanted to provide, we needed to stay!

There I was, pregnant, with no friends, and stuck living where I thought I would never be able to thrive. I was lonely, isolated, and resentful. The bitterness was almost too much. I woke up each day angry at God and scheming about how we could move. It came up in almost every conversation with Jamie. I constantly reminded my husband that I would never be able to survive somewhere this different from the land of my upbringing. I was so far removed from so much I held dear. And so began a long season of discontentment and counseling for me. I continued to remind my counselor that I had nothing left. I did not have my family, who now lived in North Carolina and traveled back and forth to Thailand. I did not have the culture that I loved so much. I had no identity outside of Christ, and I felt unknown and unloved.

I began chasing everything I could to get rid of how unsettled I felt inside. I danced in Boston for a professional company, which brought me some joy. Then I opened a dance studio in my basement. I needed something to do! Then I got spray-tan certified, and you better believe I bronzed the living daylights out of anyone I could convince to come to my dingy garage. To this day, that time was the most challenging transition I have ever made. But now I can look back and see that I would never have started Chasing Sacred were it not for feeling like I had nowhere to go with my feelings and nothing else to chase. After trying out several different avenues, I returned to that which I knew best—the pursuit of God in all seasons despite my constant loneliness and struggle with depression.

The reality began to set in that I couldn't dance anymore. I had always been a huge dreamer, and I knew that there was *one* thing I wanted to accomplish in life. That one thing was to make it in New York City as a contemporary dancer. I worked extremely hard to become that—hours in the studio learning choreography and rehearsing, and many years performing onstage. Those in the dance world say that most dancers give up entirely because it's just too hard, but I knew I had the perseverance and grit not to quit. So, after college, I moved to New York City. I spent hours and hours auditioning and showing up at every open call, waiting many more hours, and then being cut while thousands of other dancers waited their turn. I got small gigs here and there and some bigger, fun ones where I danced with different companies. I was living the dream—newly married but living in Manhattan with one of my best girlfriends, and pursuing my goals.

But it all stopped when I found out I was pregnant. I was not planning on having a baby this early in marriage, and I could not perform while pregnant. I came back to New Hampshire and spent the next year *miserable*. I remember telling my husband how resentful I was. "I did not get to do what I wanted to do! You are building your dream, and I want mine!" Over and over again, God called me to surrender both what I dreamed about and what I was chasing. He even began to change my desires. I soon found that I loved motherhood and all it had to offer. I learned over time that I preferred not traveling away from my babies but instead writing at nap time. My creative outlet had been taken from me, and I was in a new state with no friends, but I found solace in my nap-time creativity.

I struggled and struggled through the next two years, and in that time, I continued to write. My dream—the one thing I was trying so hard to pursue—had died. I wrote whatever I could, including devotionals, and I dug into God's Word. Every day I clung to Scripture to make sense of what didn't make sense to me. In my loneliness, I clung to Scripture. In my anger, I clung to Scripture. Then I began to share my writing. Around this time, I started a blog, and Chasing Sacred was born. As I posted about what I was learning, I continued to learn more and more about what I was teaching. I taught the Bible every chance I got! I spoke about it on Instagram, I took on any in-person speaking event I could do, and I even hosted workshops in my house. I knew I needed to continue learning by going to seminary. After my second son was born, I began my studies to get my master's in theology. I started to understand theology and how the parts fit into the whole. My eyes were opened to more of God's character. I finally understood how Martin Luther felt when he reportedly said,

> I study my Bible like I gather apples. First, I shake the
> whole tree that the ripest may fall. Then I shake each limb,
> and when I have shaken each limb, I shake each branch
> and every twig. Then I look under every leaf. I search
> the Bible as a whole like shaking the whole tree. Then I
> shake every limb—study book after book. Then I shake
> every branch, giving attention to the chapters. Then I
> shake every twig, or a careful study of the paragraphs and
> sentences and words and their meanings.[1]

I made it my goal to teach anyone who would listen how to study the Bible using the Inductive Bible Study method! I taught on Instagram and Facebook, and I hosted classes in my living room for my friends and family members.

Watch for Clues

During my childhood, our house was burglarized twice in one year when we were living in Thailand in a *moo ban* (neighborhood).

The second time happened while we were on vacation. Someone broke into our house and stole all sorts of things. The crime scene was obvious. Our belongings had been rifled through, drawers were pried open, and all my precious fake jewelry was burned black. Life lesson: if you ever want to test whether a piece of jewelry is real gold, you can use a lighter and put a steady flame next to it. If it is real, it will not char. Since I was a missionary kid, my jewelry was cheaper than cheap. But it was a bummer to find that it had been ruined.

Now, oblige me for a second and put on your detective spectacles. Help me use some solid reasoning to analyze this crime scene. If I began my investigation by thinking I already knew who the criminal was and looking for evidence to support my theory, I would be using deductive reasoning, moving from general to specific. Deductive reasoning does not serve us when we're investigating a crime scene . . . or studying the Bible. In Bible study, deductive reasoning looks like coming to a specific passage with the desire for it to answer a particular problem in our life. We see this when preachers or Bible teachers use a text to support their own agenda. (I have been guilty of this in the past!)

For example, a friend recently shared a story with me. She and her husband were in a public setting when another man accused her husband of doing something that he had indeed done but intended for good. She stayed silent in the middle of the gathering but then cried all night and woke up burdened, wanting God to speak. She opened her Bible and prayerfully wondered if she should call this person out in public. The passage of Scripture she randomly turned to was Deuteronomy 25:11-12: "If two men are fighting and the wife of one of them comes to rescue her husband from his assailant, and she reaches out and seizes him by his private parts, you shall cut off her hand. Show her no pity." God gave her quite the laugh that day.

Turning to a random Scripture passage and expecting it to speak to our situation is the opposite of good exegesis. I could read my own personal circumstances, time in history, and life situation into any passage of Scripture, but that doesn't mean I'll have any idea what the passage actually means.

Inductive reasoning is the opposite of deductive reasoning. It is a process that seminarians and professors alike have used since before the nineteenth century, and it is the foundation of Inductive Bible Study. Inductive reasoning in Bible study is the process of letting the evidence we find in the text lead us toward a conclusion about the purpose of the text. When I first went to Bible college, Inductive Bible Study impacted me in a way I had never experienced before. I had never heard of this way of studying the Bible, and I could not believe it was not more widely known. I felt a fire in my bones that would not be put out until I could see every man and woman be given these tools to study the Bible more effectively.

Let's apply inductive reasoning to the crime scene we discussed earlier. First, we observe the scene. For example, we could begin by noticing that the door was left wide open, the drawers were rifled through, and there was a trail of bright-orange candle wax throughout the house (true story). If we followed the trail, we could walk down the hallway and see exactly where the robber went. Then we would notice a cigarette butt left outside, and we would examine the jewelry and find fingerprints.

After we observed all these facts, we could move on to begin interpreting them. This interpretation of events might lead us to find that the candle probably meant this crime was committed at night. The cigarette butt might lead us to believe the criminal was a smoker. When we apply all these clues to the pool of suspects, we may be able to determine who the culprit was.

Inductive reasoning helps us to see what to do next with the evidence we have been given. The three-step process of Inductive

Bible Study—observation, interpretation, and application—is a slowed-down method of looking at Scripture. It is not about drawing conclusions fast, but instead it emphasizes meditating on and savoring the text.

Scholars have found that beginning by examining the clues in the text is crucial for understanding the Bible. That is why the observation part of Inductive Bible Study is so important. Observation means asking the question "What do I see?" or "What does this say?"

When I'm explaining the three steps of Inductive Bible Study further, I like using the illustration of road signs. When we come upon a road sign, the first thing we do is take notice of it and observe what it says.

In Inductive Bible Study, observation begins with outlining and marking key words in the text. This is one way to approach the process of exegesis. Jen Wilkin defines exegesis as "excavating the original meaning of a passage. Each of us is a product of the time and culture in which we live, and as such, we bring certain biases to our reading of Scripture."[2] Exegesis is trying to look at the text with clarity of vision for the original hearers' day and age. It is mining the text to discover how it was understood when it was first written. It is asking the text what it's saying in plain terms. What is the most basic meaning of the text?

Praying and asking the Lord to walk hand in hand with you as you read the Bible is a beautiful posture of surrender to start your Bible study time.

But before we even begin observation, we pray. Praying and asking the Lord to walk hand in hand with you as you read the Bible is a beautiful posture of surrender to start your Bible study time. Here's an example of the type of prayer you can pray as you begin Bible study:

Lord God,

Open my eyes to what You want me to see in this text.
Help me to have wisdom and understanding. Guide my heart
to hear Your desires. Guide my eyes to see Your truth.

May my study today be fruitful, and please multiply my
efforts. Thank You, Lord, for Your Word—and that it never
returns void!

In Jesus' name, amen.

Next, choose a passage of the Bible that you want to study, and depending on the length of the book it is in, read the whole book front to back. This might be harder with longer books like Isaiah, but it is still a great goal. If you are reading the Psalms, I recommend reading just the psalm you are studying since all of them are separate poems or songs. If it is a shorter book like Philippians, read it three times through, once out loud if you can. If reading an entire book of the Bible feels overwhelming right now, just read the surrounding chapters, and make sure to take in as much context and background as possible. Reading an entire book— once or multiple times—is not an exercise that we do to zone out and think about tonight's dinner. It is part of internalizing what we are reading with intention. After establishing the context of a Scripture passage in this way, I often urge people to find an overview of the book of the Bible they are studying, perhaps in a study Bible or online commentary. In my women's Bible study class, we also watch one of the BibleProject videos (available for free online) to familiarize ourselves with the book's overall message.

At my international school in Thailand, I took a Thai language class. It became evident from the beginning that I could do very little and still get a good grade because my Thai teachers thought I was hilarious. I vividly remember a "test" I took where I needed to read a book about a train in Thai. Instead of taking the time to learn what the words meant, I memorized the book. I also had zero comprehension because I was just reciting Thai words I remembered. I am sure you all can relate to this kind of memorization. We memorized so many things as children in a rote manner without even thinking about the meaning. Many of us approach Scripture in a similar way. We read it with very little thought about what it truly means. When we grasp the deeper meaning and allow the words to touch our hearts in a new way, we will be amazed at the power of even the most familiar Scripture passages.

Recognize His Voice

Recently, an influx of online messages and parenting information began to paralyze me. When I spoke to my kids, I began to tighten my voice. I wondered if I was damaging my children, and I thought long and hard about whether I was doing anything right. I felt like these voices from the internet were now in my head, standing in my living room. I felt shame about everything I was doing. It was dulling that voice I knew so well—the Holy Spirit.

I was getting so caught up in the technicalities of parenting that I forsook the end goal of parenting: relationship. I want to reiterate that the end goal of Bible study is a relationship with God. Please do not let learning how to study the Bible paralyze you from getting into the Word because you are so concerned about getting it "right."

For a while, I was continually pressing pause on my parenting to check in with those online voices to see if I was doing it right. And then it dawned on me. There is a reason God did not give other people's voices access to my house. There is a reason God did not give other people access to your heart and your relationship with Him. Do not let all this new information about Inductive Bible Study overwhelm you or cause you to be paralyzed when reading God's Word.

We live in a day and age where it's too easy to let social media guide us. The online world can be a huge distraction from our Bible reading. Thankfully, God has given us the power of prayer and access to the Holy Spirit so we can discern what to do when we're tempted to let the internet sweep us away. I did not cut out every wise voice giving me parenting advice, but I did stop questioning everything I was doing. I knew that the more plugged in I was to the Spirit's voice and the power of prayer (rather than online parenting forums), the more I could glean wisdom in hard moments with my kids.

Please do not let learning how to study the Bible paralyze you from getting into the Word because you are so concerned about getting it "right."

A similar dynamic is at play when I study my Bible. I've had to put strict phone habits in place during my Bible reading time. I have always found it hard to gain context from reading the Bible on my phone anyway. It doesn't take much more effort to grab a physical Bible or to open my computer to use Bible study software that has access to commentaries. I cannot stress enough that proper phone boundaries can save your Bible study. I now pull up my passages in Logos Bible Software on my computer and leave my phone on airplane mode until I finish my Bible study and get the kids off to school!

My deepest desire for you as you go through this book is that you would have confidence in the Spirit's voice as you read and delight in God's Word. That this book would not paralyze you but make you more prayerful. Here's how I like to see it: I used to call a restaurant quite often to place delivery orders. One day I called to order, and a voice on the other side said, "Mikella, is that you?"

I giggled right away. "Morgan! I thought that was you!"

In the same vein, we can have growing confidence in the Spirit's voice as we consistently test what we are learning by studying other passages in the Bible that talk about the same subject. We grow in knowing the Spirit's voice as we become more familiar with His promptings in and through His Word. I could confirm that Morgan was on the phone by testing her voice because we have a personal relationship and her voice is distinct. Be prayerful in your study and submit yourself to the Holy Spirit's guidance, and you will easily be able to recognize His voice.

Gather Background Information

After reading the entire book you're studying several times (or reading the surrounding chapters), begin by asking questions about the book as a whole before you ask questions about the specific section you're focusing on. I like to gather background information on the book as well. I usually do this by googling it or reading the book introductions in my study Bible. I try to answer these questions:

- Who was the author?
- Who was the audience?
- Who were the key characters?
- What was the author saying?
- Where did it take place?
- When was it written?
- Why was it written?
- How will it happen?

These questions will help you gain context for the entirety of the book. Taking the extra step to answer them is like sending down roots in the soil before you study. It will ground you and give you a place to begin.

Compare Translations

Comparing translations will give us a lot of insight into the words or phrases that the author used to convey what they were saying. When we compare translations we get to see different words that the translators picked, which shows us that some words can have varying meanings. Many people have a translation preference in their Bible reading, but the most helpful thing we can do in Bible study is to compare translations to get a greater understanding of the author's intent in writing the passage.

Zoom In

After you've answered these questions, it's time to zoom in on the specific passage you're studying. Even if you have already read the entire book, read a few paragraphs before and after the passage one more time. Make sure you understand it in context. Then you can begin marking up the passage.

I always highlight key words, repeated words, and linking words as I uncover what a passage of Scripture is about.

Key Words

Start by looking for key words in the passage. Key words help us to understand the meaning of the text and point us toward the theme of the passage. They may be repeated words but don't necessarily have to be. As you read through the passage, ask yourself, *What is the idea that the author is trying to convey?* Marking up key words can help you discover the purpose of what you are reading. It helps you connect with the text in a kinesthetic way that engages your brain. Once you read through the passage a couple of times, you will be surprised at how these key words pop out to you. You will also be surprised at how highlighting the key words helps unlock the meaning of the passage. They don't have to be big theological terms, but they are always significant to the passage. If these key words were omitted, the purpose or point of the passage would be lost. If you read the book of 1 John, for example, you will see the word *know* over and over. That is one of many key words in the book.

I also find it helpful to mark some key words in the same color or manner every single time I see them! This means I have a key graph that helps me to determine how to mark up my Bible. (See visual below.) You can copy mine or make up your own!

HOW TO MARK UP YOUR BIBLE

Mark Key Words

△ God
♡ Lord
☐ Jesus
◀ Gospel
✿ Holy Spirit
👑 Kingdom
☆ Father
••• Son
✗ Devil/Satan

Highlight/Mark:

He when referring to God
— Pronouns
Repeated words
🕐 References to time
⟨⟹ Contrasts
Introductions and conclusions
Geographical locations
*When reading an Epistle, color
the author in one color; and
the audience in a second color

God's Discipline Proves His Love

12 Therefore, since we are surrounded by such a huge crowd of witnesses to the life of faith, let us strip off every weight that slows us down, especially the sin that so easily trips us up. And let us run with endurance the race God has set before us. [2] We do this by keeping our eyes on Jesus, the champion who initiates and perfects our faith.* Because of the joy* awaiting him, he endured the cross, disregarding its shame. Now he is seated in the place of honor beside God's throne. [3] Think of all the hostility he endured from sinful people;* then you won't become weary and give up. [4] After all, you have not yet given your lives in your struggle against sin.

[5] And have you forgotten the encouraging words God spoke to you as his children?* He said,

"My child,* don't make light of the LORD's discipline,
    and don't give up when he corrects you.
[6] For the LORD disciplines those he loves,
    and he punishes each one he accepts as his child."*

[7] As you endure this divine discipline, remember that God is treating you as his own children. Who ever heard of a child who is never disciplined by its father? [8] If God doesn't discipline you as he does all of his children, it means that you are illegitimate and are not really his children at all. [9] Since we respected our earthly fathers who disciplined us, shouldn't we submit even more to the discipline of the Father of our spirits, and live forever?*

[10] For our earthly fathers disciplined us for a few years, doing the best they knew how. But God's discipline is always good for us, so that we might share in his holiness. [11] No discipline is enjoyable while it is happening—it's painful! But afterward there will be a peaceful harvest of right living for those who are trained in this way. [12] So take a new grip with your tired hands and strengthen your weak knees. [13] Mark out a straight path for your feet so that those who are weak and lame will not fall but become strong.

Repeated Words

Repeated words come up more than once in a passage of Scripture to help us discover its meaning.

They can be in a row, as in this example:

Holy, holy, holy is the LORD Almighty;
    the whole earth is full of his glory.
ISAIAH 6:3

Words don't have to fall back-to-back to count as repeated words, though. Here's an example of a passage that contains repeated words, just not next to each other.

Remember, dear brothers and sisters, that few of you were **wise** in the **world's** eyes or **powerful** or wealthy when **God** called you. Instead, **God chose things** the **world considers** foolish in order to **shame** those who think they are **wise**. And **he chose things** that are **powerless** to **shame** those who are **powerful**. **God chose things** despised by the **world**, things counted as **nothing** at all, and used them to bring to **nothing** what the **world considers** important. As a result, no one can ever boast in the presence of **God**.
I CORINTHIANS 1:26-29, NLT

Highlighting repeated words is important because it helps us get to the intent of the passage and find out what truth God is conveying to us. Again, we are trying to answer the question "What does this say?" Underneath this question is the assumption that we want to understand what God is saying. Remember the story of when my house in Thailand was robbed and how we must examine clues to understand the meaning of a Bible passage? Well, marking up these words helps us to discover what the passage is about.

Linking Words

Linking words are also known as conjunctions. Some examples of linking words you'll come across are *because*, *therefore*, *but*, and *so*. These small but mighty words help us discover how sentences and thoughts connect. When we see a *because*, for example, we know the author is about to explain the reason for something. When we come across a *therefore*, we know the author is about to let us know the implication or result of what was just said. If we see a *but*, we know the following thought will present a contrast with the preceding thought. Sometimes the small word *so* will indicate the result of the statement before it. Let's look at the connecting words in 2 Corinthians 5:14: "For Christ's love compels us, *because* we are convinced that one died for all, and *therefore* all died" (emphasis added). The reason Paul is compelled to preach to others is that he is convinced Christ died for all. The implication of Jesus' death for us is that we also died to ourselves. Connecting words like these alert us to the reasoning and intent of statements in the passage.

Time and Location

We also want to pay attention to words that indicate time or location. This is important because we can really understand the passage better if we understand where in the world the writing took place and what time period it was in. We also can gain insight if we think through references to time that talk about whether something was done slowly, or fast. It's easy to overlook these words, but the biblical authors chose to include them for a reason. Mark's Gospel is often called the action-packed Gospel because the word *immediately* appears forty-one times.[3]

Whenever we come across references to time, it's a good idea to highlight them. In this psalm, when we highlight time, we gain some understanding of what Moses was saying about God's character and His eternal nature: "For *a thousand years* in your sight are but as *yesterday* when it is past, or as a watch in the *night*" (Psalm 90:4, ESV, emphasis added).

I often highlight location or geographical words in one color and time words in another. Understanding geographical location can help us see when events have progressed, whether Jesus was traveling somewhere, or whether another biblical character left home to go somewhere else. Here is an example of a location reference:

"With her two daughters-in-law she left the place where she had been living and *set out on the road* that would take them *back to the land of Judah*" (Ruth 1:7, emphasis added). In this passage and in the context of Ruth 1 we see that Naomi left the land of Moab to return home to Israel. We cannot fully understand what was happening in the passage until we investigate these locations and the significance of these places during the time the book was written.

Contrasts and Comparisons

A contrast is when two opposites show us a reality, illustrate something, or teach us something. In the following passage, you can see the word *but*, which often signals that we are dealing with a contrast. "The mouth of the righteous is a fountain of life, but the mouth of the wicked conceals violence" (Proverbs 10:11). The mouth of the righteous in this passage is contrasted with the mouth of the wicked! It is useful to picture what each of these are likened to within the contrast. When I imagine the righteous person's mouth, I picture water bubbling out of a beautiful well that is used to quench thirst. The mouth of the wicked is the opposite of bubbling—it is concealing or hiding violence. The vivid contrasting imagery in this verse makes the writer's point even more powerful.

Comparisons are another device that helps us to understand an idea or visualize a lesson. When my husband turned forty, I threw a huge birthday bash for him and compiled videos of his friends saying their favorite things about him. One of the questions I asked in the video was "If Jamie were an animal, what would he be?" Without comparing their answers, all his friends said, "Gorilla." The fact that everyone compared my husband to a gorilla still makes me laugh. For our purposes, a comparison is when one thing is described as similar to something else. The word *like* or *as* is often used to signal that two ideas are being compared.

In James 1:22-25 we read, "Do not merely listen to the word, and so deceive yourselves. Do what it says. Anyone who listens to the word but does not do what it says is like someone who looks at his face in a mirror and, after looking at himself, goes away and immediately forgets what he looks like. But whoever looks intently into the perfect law that gives freedom, and continues in it—not forgetting what they have heard, but doing it—they will be blessed in what they do."

In James's day, mirrors were often made out of polished metal. When people looked in a mirror, they had to stare intently in order to examine themselves. This is the way we should read God's Word—and just as importantly, we should remember and apply what it shows us and exhorts us to do.

Make Lists

A really fun way to observe the text is through list-making. Do you see a list of the characteristics of God? Write them in the margins of your Bible! I will give you an example. Exodus 34:6-7 says, "And [the LORD] passed in front of Moses, proclaiming, 'The LORD, the LORD, the compassionate and gracious God, slow to anger, abounding in love and faithfulness, maintaining love to thousands, and forgiving wickedness, rebellion and sin. Yet he does not leave the guilty unpunished; he punishes the children and their children for the sin of the parents to the third and fourth generation.'"

Characteristics of God:

- compassionate
- gracious
- slow to anger
- abounding in love
- abounding in faithfulness
- maintaining love to thousands
- forgiving wickedness, rebellion, and sin
- does not leave the guilty unpunished
- punishes the children and their children for the sin of the parents to the third and fourth generation

Write Down Questions

I love to write down any questions I have of the text while I am studying. This helps me to keep track of my interests and remember ideas that I want to further investigate. Remember, the more curious you are, the more you will learn! Are there names you would like to look up later? What do you not understand or what do you find confusing in this passage?

Notice Atmosphere

I find it helpful to take note of the atmosphere of the passage or section of Scripture I'm studying. What emotions were the characters feeling? Were they joyful or discouraged? Were they experiencing a spiritual struggle?

Bible Charting

Create an Outline

When I first learned about the Inductive Bible Study process, one of the biggest things I took away was that the headings, subheadings, and titles in our modern Bibles were put in by the translators. This means we shouldn't rely on paragraph or section breaks when we're studying the Bible. As a theology student, one of the first steps my class was tasked with was creating our own Bible study outline. The first thing we did was print out a book of the Bible with no chapter headings or titles and learn to create our own. This ensured that we could make our own outline without being influenced by the translators' headings and subheadings. The process helped us to uncover the theme or purpose of the passages. I learned that I could section off the Scriptures by discovering their themes and by identifying the key words and repeated words.

Remember, our goal is to discover the original author's intent. This is one of the first steps in the Inductive Bible Study method because it is again helping us look at the book as a whole and gather background information for the entirety of the book. When you are looking into how to section out the book, do what is natural *to you*. Where do you feel like the author changes the topic or pivots away from what they were talking about?

Here's how I recommend outlining a passage or the book you are studying:

1. Divide the passage into sections by thought units.
2. Summarize each section in a sentence. This helps you figure out the main point of the passage and condense it to internalize what you are reading.
3. Next to that sentence, write a one-to-three-word title

for the section. It should be related to what you feel the overall theme of the passage is. Base your title on all the key words and repeated words that you have already marked up.

4. Write the purpose of the passage you are reading at the top or bottom of what you have read. This helps you clarify your thoughts as you seek to understand the purpose of the entire book by looking at the parts.

Below, I've included an example of what it could look like to follow these steps:

SCRIPTURE PASSAGE: LUKE 1:1-15		
Section	**Summary**	**Title**
Luke 1:1-4	Luke records the truth so that we may know.	An Orderly Account
Luke 1:5-7	Elizabeth and Zechariah are righteous but without a child.	Without Child
Luke 1:8-15	An angel appears to Zechariah and announces great tidings.	An Angel Announces
Purpose of the Passage: Recording an orderly account of the events leading up to Christ's birth.		

Ask Two Things

Observation in Inductive Bible Study asks the questions "What does it say?" and "What do I see?"

We begin with being humble and curious, asking questions of the text. "Without a curiosity to know the truth with increasing depth and a fresh perspective, the motivation to study God's Word would quickly evaporate, and Bible study would become a lifeless burden without expectation and joy. However, curiosity must be harnessed to provide real benefit in Bible study, and inquiry must work in concert with the inductive method if the engine of the mind is to run with efficiency and power."[4]

When we observe the text, we examine the clues without concluding anything yet. The key to the inductive method is to slow down and soak in the text. This part happens when we mark up our Bibles, make lists, and try to see what God is communicating to us. Observation leads us to discover authorial intent. It helps us to understand the "why" behind every section of Scripture and the motivation behind the words.

Paraphrase the Text

I want to talk about the power of paraphrasing, which is an essential step in the observation process. As we search the text for what is already there, we want to understand what it's saying. When I began teaching people how to do Inductive Bible Study, I quickly realized that paraphrasing the text is a surefire way to comprehend it. One of the goals of Bible study is to internalize what we are learning, and paraphrasing helps us do that. Often I automatically paraphrase when I ask the question "What was the author saying?" (See next section.) By putting what the author is saying into my own words, I am answering this question and gaining understanding.

Ask Questions

The next step is to ask specific questions about the Scripture passage. With the background questions in mind, we must then seek to move toward questions that draw out more details from the text.

People in the Inductive Bible Study world call this the 5 *W*'s and an *H*: Who, What, Where, When, Why, and How?
These are the specific questions I ask:

- Who was the author?
- Who was the audience?
- Who were the key characters?
- What was the author saying?
- Where did it take place?
- When was it written?
- Why was it written?
- How will it happen?

Did you know that asking the right questions in the observation process will lead you to interpretation? It's pretty neat. I love how Richard Alan Fuhr and Andreas Köstenberger describe this process: "Interpretive questions primarily function as a bridge between observation and interpretation, although questions can play a role throughout the entire inductive process. Essentially, this means that observations prompt interpretive questions (observation having revealed the interpretive issues inherent in the text), and as those questions are answered, the interpretation of the text will naturally ensue."[5]

Who was the author?

Identifying the author of the book we are studying can be very helpful in grasping some of the significance of a passage. It sets the scene for the book by identifying a real flesh-and-blood individual. It lends itself to further understanding how to interpret and apply. Based on what we know of the author's life and other writings, we can draw conclusions about how to interpret and apply a passage.

Who was the audience?

Identifying the audience is crucial to biblical interpretation because it helps us to gauge what issues the audience might have been struggling with or what particular admonishment the audience needed. Understanding the audience's culture, ideologies, or historical/cultural context helps us to understand the book we are studying better.

Who were the key characters?

Identifying the key characters in the passage will help provide understanding about what is going on. Write down any names or people mentioned in the surrounding passages. Is the passage talking about God? Or the Spirit? Be vigilant in marking down any characters in the text.

What was the author saying?

As I mention above, paraphrasing is a powerful tool that helps us discover the intent of a passage. Reiterating the passage in our own words is an important way to help us understand what the author was saying. It causes us to think about the information and synthesize it into our own words, thereby helping us grasp its intent.

Where did it take place?

It is important to understand the setting of a passage because it sets the scene for our understanding of the passage as a whole. What was life like in the location we are studying? Were there certain challenges at the time? What was the socioeconomic status of the individuals in the text? Just as a novel begins by grounding us in where it was written, knowing the location of a Bible passage helps us to grasp its meaning in a broader way.

When was it written?

The historical context of a passage matters. The events of the Bible happened at a certain time in history. This means that understanding the time in history in which it was written adds meaning and breadth to any passage of the Bible. Grasping the time in history is significant because it leads us to a well-rounded understanding of what certain words, phrases, or symbols in the text mean.

Why was it written?

We want to get to the bottom of why the passage is in the Bible. Is it instructing us in some way? Is it telling a story about the nation of Israel? Is it explaining a theological principle? Is it addressing a problem in the church in the first century? Is it showing us more about God's character? When I try to grasp why a book was written, I take into account the purpose of the passage I'm reading. In writing down why it was written, I am one step closer to the passage's purpose. In the "why" I often discover whether God is communicating knowledge to me about a theological truth, a moral truth, a biographical truth, or even a historical truth.

How will it happen?

How will this come about? Has it happened yet? Is it promised to a specific group, or does it apply to all of God's people? Is this passage talking about a specific event that will happen in the future? If so, when and where will this event take place? Or is it talking about an ideological concept that will take place when we pursue Christ (for example, experiencing agape love)? How will this concept come about? Looking at how a passage points us forward or backward can help us know how to apply the text.

Observe the Truth

In my current hometown, many of us love to dine at a quaint little restaurant in the middle of nowhere. The restaurant's claim to fame is its resemblance to the grandmother's cottage from the story "Little Red Riding Hood." I am sure you are familiar with these lines from the story:

"Grandmother! What big ears you have," exclaims Little Red Riding Hood.

"The better to hear you with, my dear," replies the wolf disguised as her grandmother.

"But, Grandmother! What big eyes you have."

"The better to see you with, my dear."

Finally Little Red Riding Hood says, "What big teeth you have!"

The wolf responds with his final intentions. "The better to eat you with, my dear."

Little Red Riding Hood makes many observations in this part of the story. She begins by noting the physical characteristics of the wolf in front of her. As her statements progress, she gets closer and closer to the truth. Little Red Riding Hood evaluates the wolf's appearance, which leads her to the reality of the wolf's desires.

As we learn to study the Bible, we must observe the text in the same way Little Red Riding Hood observes the wolf. Once we have thoroughly observed the content of the passage, it's time to move on to the second part of Inductive Bible Study: interpretation. Observation and interpretation are closely interconnected. In the observation stage, we answer the question "What is this passage about?" The interpretation stage will show us how to answer the question "What does this mean?" In the next chapter, we'll learn how to take the first step in accurate interpretation: fully understanding the context of a passage.

9

UNCOVER CONTEXT

MY HUSBAND, JAMIE, a big, burly-shouldered man, captured my heart when he told me of his love for missions. One of the first times I met Jamie, he shared about the colorful country of Guatemala. We found common ground over the fact that I had grown up in Thailand, and he and a board of directors had started an orphanage in Guatemala called Little Lambs International. I remember one of our first mission trips together (along with six other dudes) back when we were dating. We visited the town of Antigua, known for its mountains, colorful houses, and cobblestone streets. We had each gone off to explore on our own, and when we returned, we had each bought each other a coffee. Whew! Romance at its finest! This sealed the deal on my end.

We worked all day constructing the building that would someday house some of the children he had a vision for. At this point in time, the grounds had been purchased and cleared, but we still had to get to work constructing the mission house and individual homes that my sweet, visionary husband had dreamed up with the Lord. As I watched his heart expand for the people he was serving and his desire to see these children taken care of, I knew we shared a love of living on mission for God's Kingdom. One of my favorite parts of his vision was how Little Lambs was different from the traditional orphanage model: it was a non-adoptive orphanage where the kids would be raised in the Word of God in their own designated house family with a mother and father figure. Once the kids grew up, they would be equipped to enact change for their own country.

Having grown up in a missionary family myself, I also love the idea of integrating outreach into our own family. Our eight-year-old has already been to Guatemala seven times, as we see these yearly trips to help at the orphanage as an integral part of our kids' upbringing. This legacy is one way I can see how God cares about my history and its impact on my kids' lives.

I remember asking Jamie how they chose the town for the orphanage, and he said the decision took a lot of research. A missionary named Ryan had lived in Guatemala for many years and had investigated the area extensively, including whether there were other orphanages serving the population. Ryan had specifically searched for a place where an orphanage would have the greatest impact on the community. He believed they couldn't just build it anywhere without considering the landmarks and the people nearby. If the orphanage was to serve its purpose, it could not be isolated from its location. The land needed to be chosen to match the need.

Remember the Bigger Picture

This story of selecting the right spot for the orphanage can remind us of how to read the Bible. We often isolate Bible verses, believing that the purpose of a verse can be separated from the surrounding passages. But like the team building the orphanage, we need to remember the bigger picture. A Bible verse is not an island, alone in an enormous sea of water. If we are going to read well, we must take note of the context.

Have you ever received a text that made no sense because you didn't have enough information? The other day, I sent my friend Stacey a one-off humorous text about dinner the night before. "Don't forget the restaurant is fine dining." I snapped a picture of my son wearing my blonde extensions and made a joke about how I'd looked that night. The only problem was that I had messaged the wrong Stacey. Without experiencing last night's dinner, she could not understand my text! When we ignore the surrounding passages in the Bible, it's as if—like Stacey—we got a text message about an event we weren't even at. We aren't able to appreciate how the verses build on each other and how the context brings further insight to the story, capturing the themes that run throughout the Bible's pages.

One verse that's often taken out of context is Matthew 18:20: "Where two or three are gathered together in my name, there am I in the midst of them" (KJV). I have heard people bring this verse up many times in a small group, Bible study, or church service. Last time I heard this verse mentioned, the person was implying that because more than two people were present, God was promising to be there among them. The only problem is this could also imply that if someone is alone, God is not around. The common misinterpretation is problematic because it ignores the context of the passage. If you read Matthew 18:15-20, you will discover that this passage deals with sin in the church. It also provides a step-by-step guide to dealing with conflict in the church. When someone sins, you should address them privately (verse 15). Next, two to three trusted people should confront them (verse 16). If they still won't listen, you can bring the church leaders with you to talk to the person once again (verse 17). The goal in all of this is repentance and restoration. Verse 20 comforts us by pointing to Jesus' presence in the midst of church discipline and conflict when we follow the steps that Scripture gives us. The whole purpose of the passage is restoration in the church.

A practical way of understanding this verse's context is to first read the passages surrounding Matthew 18:20. Looking up a summary of the themes present in this section of the book of Matthew can also be helpful. Researching the context before you read helps a lot with interpretation.

Literary Context

As Gregory Koukl explains simply, "Never read a Bible verse."[1] He is not saying we can't *ever* read a verse on its own. But he *is* saying that we should seek to read the surrounding passages as well because many times context is the key to unlocking understanding. When I refer to context, the first thing on my mind is the authorial intent, which is discovered by studying the literary, historical, and cultural context of a verse or passage. Literary context includes the passages surrounding the verse in question and where it fits in the big story of redemptive history that runs throughout the entire Bible. Robert H. Stein defines context as "the communicative intent of the author found in the words, sentences, paragraphs, and chapters surrounding a passage."[2] When we think about the literary context, we want to start by examining the words, phrases, and passages surrounding the verse we are focused on. Then we can consider the book of the Bible we're in, and then the whole metanarrative—the entirety of the Bible. Examining the literary context also has a lot to do with genre, which I dedicate an entire chapter to later in the book.

When we do not read a verse or a passage in its literary context, we can misinterpret and misapply it. In my women's Bible study recently, we had a discussion that perfectly illustrates the importance of context. We were discussing a problematic situation in our community, and one woman reminded us that, according to the Bible, we could pour hot coals on our enemy's head (see Romans 12:20). Although I did not know what that meant, it sounded pretty gruesome. We all began laughing at the thought. When we looked up the verse, we laughed even harder. The context of the verse tells us that by *being kind*, we will figuratively pour hot coals on an enemy's head. If we had just taken the verse at face value without examining the context, we would have misinterpreted it. Right before this verse, after all, God reminds us that vengeance is His! Look at Romans 12:18-19, which comes right before the burning coals verse:

> If it is possible, as far as it depends on you, live at peace
> with everyone. Do not take revenge, my dear friends, but
> leave room for God's wrath, for it is written: "It is mine
> to avenge; I will repay," says the Lord.

It's only then that we read verse 20:

> If your enemy is hungry, feed him;
>   if he is thirsty, give him something to drink.
> In doing this, you will heap burning coals on his head.

When we read the whole passage, it's clear that the true meaning of God's Word is the opposite of what it seems to be when we just read the second part of verse 20 on its own.

Historical Context

Similarly, we need to understand the historical context when studying a passage of Scripture. I appreciate the way Jen Wilkin describes historical context by comparing the Bible to the city of Rome. As she describes it, modern-day Rome actually sits on top of ancient Rome.[3] She explains that when a Roman homeowner wants to do some type of renovation, they have to seriously consider what is underneath their home.

> Rome does not allow its residents to dig without regard for its rich and relevant history. All modern-day building must be done with care, recognizing that its current inhabitants live in a context that is much bigger than the short period of time they will dwell there. . . . Like the modern-day residents of Rome, modern-day Christians must handle our Bibles with much the same understanding. Modern-day Christians inherit a faith that is built on the foundations of that which has come before. We, too, must occupy a modern space while maintaining an ancient perspective."[4]

Similarly, we need to understand that the events of Scripture happened at a certain time in history and acknowledge what was going on politically, socially, and geographically at that time period. To fully understand the historical context, we must learn who the original author was, why the book was written, and who the book was written for.

Cultural Context

I have a distinct memory of the limbs of a doll lying on the dirt ground of a village on the border of Myanmar. The doll looked out of place in a village where children played with rubber bands, shoes, and tires for toys.

Peeking through the cracks of the bamboo floor to the dirt below, I eyed the doll's arm and head. The Christmas gift my parents had given to a little girl in this refugee camp had lasted a mere twelve hours before the arms were plucked off and the head pulled out. The body was nowhere to be found. After dismembering the doll, the girl returned to the "toys" she usually played with as what was left of the doll lay motionless on the dirt floor. No one else in the village had a doll, so it was quickly discarded as its new owner moved on to play a more familiar game.

We tend to isolate the parts from the whole when it comes to Scripture. Just as the doll's body was separated from its limbs, we often take the Bible away from the cultural context that teaches us how to interpret it.

When we're reading the Old Testament, we must place ourselves in the ancient Near East, which informed its writing. When studying the New Testament, we must place ourselves in the Greco-Roman world. As twenty-first-century Westerners, we are so far removed from the period and culture of the Bible's writing that we might not be able to picture what is happening in the text unless we're willing to do some work.

I can still remember the day my disgruntled friend, Mint, yelled at me during recess. I was probably nine. As usual, we were leaving the cafeteria—the place where we ate our burning-hot Thai noodle soup on 100-degree days—and walking toward the outdoor *sala* (the open-air gym area where I spent hours and hours playing Chinese jump rope). I was joking around and instinctively rubbed Mint's head with my hand. She stopped in her tracks and shouted a string of not-so-kind words at me.

Pretend for a second you are an onlooker. What do you think happened here? What made my friend so angry? If you overheard her yelling and your cultural background was not Thai, you might not understand. Perhaps you'd think Mint was upset because I was being overly affectionate. But that wasn't it. Thankfully, I quickly realized what I had done wrong. "I am *so* sorry, Mint!" I apologized profusely, not skipping a beat because I knew I should not have touched her head. To a Thai person, the head is the most sacred part of the body; it is extremely disrespectful to touch someone's head. While the head is the most esteemed body part, the feet are considered dirty. Therefore, I would have gotten a similar response if I had pointed my feet at her or stepped over her body (or head!) while playing a game.

Here is what I am getting at: culture is important. When we understand the culture of the author and the audience in biblical times, we can understand an important part of the context. For example, someone might read 1 Corinthians 11:3-16 and conclude that women should wear head coverings. Before we all adopt this cultural practice, though, we would do well to ask ourselves: What did the head covering represent in Paul's culture, and what does it represent today? Do these two meanings align? Why did Paul tell women to cover their heads?

Here is one important hermeneutical principle I have learned: a passage of Scripture cannot mean to us what it did not mean to its original audience. Understanding that the Bible was written in a certain cultural climate helps us to interpret it accurately. When we come up against challenging cultural differences, we must start with this baseline hermeneutical principle. Our interpretation should be based on what the passage meant to the original audience. The principles gleaned from the text can then be applied to our time in history and our own culture.

"You really shouldn't talk to your mom like that," my Thai best friend Jinny scolded me at age twelve. "It is very disrespectful to someone who is an authority over you." As a young Thai girl, she saw the world through her own cultural lens. It was very different from the American household I grew up in, where we were allowed to speak our minds. When I was a child, it seemed everything in Thai culture was based on authority. The Thai language uses different words to greet someone depending on their seniority or measure of respect. We would greet others with a gesture called a *wai*, where we bowed our head and positioned our hands with palms together. The *wai* looks different depending on the age and status of the person you are greeting. Thailand is a collectivist honor and shame culture, more similar to first-century Palestine than today's Western world, which is very individualistic.

A passage of Scripture cannot mean to us what it did not mean to its original audience.

Interestingly enough, I remember Jinny scolding me again when I was fifteen for being too affectionate with my boyfriend in public. She told me her mother told her to admonish me because many of the older women were talking, and it could cause embarrassment to my family. But as an individualistic American, my well-being was not wrapped up in whether or not I brought honor or shame to my family. Jinny's observation was not alarming to me because my cultural background was so different from hers. In their book *Misreading Scripture with Western Eyes*, E. Randolph Richards and Brandon O'Brien point out, "Members of collectivist cultures make decisions based on the counsel of elders—parents, aunts or uncles. The highest goal and virtue in this sort of culture is supporting the community. This makes people happy (*makarios*)."[5]

E. Randolph Richards and Richard James discuss the cultural context of Joseph and his coat of many colors: "I easily assume the whole story is about him, almost turning it into a fable about how a young man left home, overcame adversity, and found success. Worse, the way I read the story had the Bible reinforcing capitalism and the American dream. When I do this, I miss a lot of what the Bible is saying. I think I know the story. Joseph is Jacob's favorite son, and Jacob gives him a gift. Right there, I have focused on two individuals. This is actually a kinship (family) story."[6] Richards and James explain how it's easy to make assumptions about a text because of our culture. When we do this, we are making the text mean something that it did not mean to the original audience, and therefore we do not fully understand it. In the collectivist culture in which it was written, the story of Joseph was about family relationships, honor and shame. Reading the story and focusing on the way those themes are woven throughout gives us a deeper understanding of the meaning.

When we take into account the cultural and historical context of Scripture, it allows us to identify the predominant themes. What is being explicitly stated, and which themes might have been implicitly clear to readers in ancient times but not to us?

Every book of the Bible is multilayered and multifaceted, and it's important to pay attention to all the themes it contains. But in the interpretation stage of Bible study, we really want to discover what the author intended for the audience to glean from the passage. What was the purpose behind what the author was writing? As R. C. Sproul puts it, "The problem of the influence of the twenty-first-century mindset is a far more formidable obstacle to accurate biblical interpretation than is the problem of the conditioning of ancient culture."[7] The conditioning of ancient culture means that the cultural context of the Bible—including the original languages and cultures and the specific historical events within it—can sometimes be less of an obstacle to accurate biblical interpretation than the twenty-first-century mindset with which each of us grew up.

When I moved to New Hampshire, I unknowingly entered a hunting culture! The problem was, I was unaware of what hunting culture entailed and how prevalent it was. I was invited to dinner at a dear friend's house and observed a plastic reindeer in their yard. The reindeer had a bull's-eye on its body, which I ignored. I giddily exclaimed to the hosts that I, too, wanted a reindeer to display in my yard for Christmas and that my unfestive husband did not love the idea of elaborate Christmas decor throughout our yard. I enjoyed the whole shebang: twinkle lights, reindeer, a sleigh, and maybe some of those blow-up penguins!

After my kind hosts had finished laughing at my mistake, they explained the reindeer had a purpose, and it was not a Christmas-related purpose. The reindeer was meant for shooting practice. The big round bull's-eye was meant to help them hit the heart. I realized I had entered a culture that I had no framework for. The only context I had for a yard animal of that size was Christmas decor. If I had applied Bible study principles of understanding context to this reindeer, I might have been slower to assume it was a holiday lawn ornament!

The Heart of God's Message

When we think about understanding a passage of Scripture, we can picture an arrow aimed at the bull's-eye heart of the passage: the purpose and meaning of the text. To hit the bull's-eye, we must understand the content of the surrounding rings. As I mentioned, I knew nothing about hunting until I moved to New

Hampshire—and now my middle son, Barkley, is obsessed with hunting. He has a bow and arrow and a target. He wants to become a skilled hunter, so he practices hitting the bull's-eye. Similarly, the heart of God's message is our main focus when we study the Bible, but the surrounding rings matter too. The outside ring represents the entirety of the Bible (the metanarrative) and its historical and cultural context; the next ring in represents the book that the verse comes from and its literary genre; the ring inside that represents the passage of Scripture, and the dot in the middle represents the heart of the passage.

Outside ring: the metanarrative/historical and cultural context
Second ring: the book of the Bible/literary genre
Third ring: the passage of Scripture
Dot in the middle: the heart of the passage

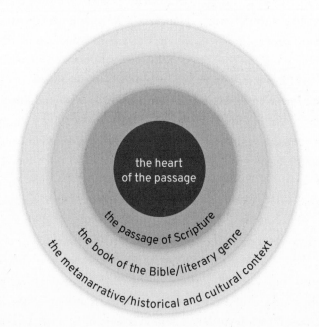

When reading Scripture, we must be attentive to what God is attentive to. Fitting my own agenda into the pages of Scripture and reading it as a means of understanding myself is easy for me to do. Thinking about what God is actually communicating through His Word takes a whole lot more discipline. I have many cares, but are they the cares of Christ? Instead of orienting the text around my personal circumstances, I need to orient myself around God's Word.

Keep Christ Center

In our biblical studies, we can become so concerned about being seen or finding ourselves in the text that it's easy to miss Christ altogether. But when we hit the bull's-eye of the passage, we will always find Christ there. It is an amazing thing to not only find Jesus in the pages of Scripture, but to be comforted and encouraged by His words and presence! Scripture transforms us.

Staying Christ-centered in our biblical studies is one of the easiest ways to avoid false teaching. The Bible has one unified message that continually points to Christ's work on our behalf. Our heart's response to what Christ did should be to worship Him and be transformed by Him. God's grace has reconciled us to Him and enabled us to be His friends—and to draw others into His grace. As He works in our hearts, we should seek to be unified as one body, the church.

Throughout the Bible, we continue to see that the greatest possible blessing is to be joined with Christ. Our union with Christ changes everything and beckons us to recognize that because of our salvation, we have received every possible spiritual benefit. A quick look at the first chapter of Ephesians, and I am blown away by what I see: in Christ, we have all the blessings that we could ever desire. Here is a glimpse of the amazing promises of Ephesians 1:1-14: Paul says that in Christ we have every spiritual blessing in the heavenly places (verse 3), we are chosen as holy and blameless (verse 4), we are predestined in love (verses 4-5), we receive redemption and forgiveness (verse 7), we are given wisdom and insight (verse 8), and He unites all things to Him and in Him (verse 10). I love what the *ESV Gospel Transformation Study Bible* says about this passage: "Our entire blessedness—our victory, our happiness, our hope—is bound up in our being bound to Christ. How foolish, and ultimately disappointed, are those who stoop to drink from any other fountain."[8] When we drink of the Word of God daily, we are placing ourselves in proximity to these blessings. We are deepening our understanding of what Christ did for us and what it looks like to live in light of that. But remember—we are not worshiping our Bible reading or our knowledge of God. Instead we are looking to the Word of God to learn more about our union with Christ so that we can love the God of the Bible.

To keep Christ at the center of my studies, I have found it beneficial to ask myself the following questions about any passage of Scripture I read:

- How does this relate to the gospel?
- What is the practical application of this gospel truth?
- Where does Christ's life, death, and resurrection fit into what I just learned or am learning?

If you are having a hard time finding Christ in an Old Testament passage, think through whether Christ is being typified in an Old Testament character or whether the passage is foreshadowing Christ or prophesying about Him. Or maybe it contains a promise that will be fulfilled in Christ. Or maybe you can gather information from the passage about God's character or the way God relates to His people.

When I have experienced confusing times in my life, I have

looked to the Scriptures to gain clarity. When my husband and I were searching for a church home during our early years of marriage, I felt very confused. We hopped around for a while and finally landed on a church, but I did not feel settled. I kept telling my husband that I was not sure we should stay there. I remember praying over and over again for clarity. We finally visited the church we still go to now. The first sermon we heard there was on the exact passage of Scripture I was studying. The next week, the pastor talked about a book I was currently reading. And the week after that, as I was feeling called into ministry, the pastor's wife asked me if she could plug me into the women's ministry and how she could support me in the church. I was shocked! God confirmed that this was the church for us three times: through the Word, through a book, and then through the pastor's wife.

Many times the path is not that clear, and instead we find that we are being called to trust, know, and love Christ rather than make one specific decision. Really, Christ is all the clarity we need. Instead of a clear path forward, I have always been surprised by how many times God's Word has urged me to walk the path of faith and to live righteously amid uncertainty. Often I find solace in knowing and loving Christ and trusting His character. Rather than giving me step-by-step instructions, God turns me to His promises and reminds me that I can trust Him in all things. Sometimes God urges me to focus on something I can do, but more often He reminds me of what Christ did for me. He invites me to obey in response to that.

If I ever find myself confused in my Bible reading about what a passage means, I do a few things:

- Ask the Lord to reveal through prayer what I am not seeing or understanding.
- Go back and study the context more in-depth.

- Look to a commentary to find what people far smarter than I have said about the passage.
- Find a passage of Scripture that speaks more clearly on the same topic.
- Review the genre of the passage, then read it again to see if it makes more sense.
- Follow cross-references, or check the study notes.

In the end, don't learn how to study the Bible just to add it to your résumé or to spar with others in a religious debate. Don't read the Bible just to gain merit. Read the Bible for communion with God. Opening up the Bible is about relationship. When you check in with your friends via text messaging, your texts ping off a cell phone tower and then appear on their phones. Similarly, your prayers connect to a real God who responds through His Word. To know Him, we have His Word! To love Him, we have His Word! To be with Him, we get to open up His living and active Word. God is our life, and God Himself saves us. We can encounter the God of the Bible! We want to know more of who God is and to grow in our love of Him. That's the ultimate goal of diving deep into Scripture.

10

IDENTIFY GENRE

ONE OF MY CHILDREN'S favorite things to do at the library is to find Schnoozer. Schnoozer is a long-nosed stuffed doll that remains hidden among the shelves until a child playing the game finds him. Whoever finds Schnoozer wins the prize of a new book that they get to keep. So far, my family has won the likes of the Hardy Boys, *The Nutcracker*, and more. We have had all-out tantrums because one child finds Schnoozer, much to the dismay of my other kids. Schnoozer is often found squeezed between different literary genres. Recently, as we were searching for Schnoozer, my eldest son read one of the signs on the shelf. "Is fiction the real one or not the real one?" he asked. I explained to him that nonfiction is a true story, and fiction is make-believe.

We grow up ingesting all sorts of literary genres without even realizing it. Literary genres are classifications of literature in distinct styles, such as fairy tales, dramas, and romances. We watch and read content in these categories without a thought about the genre. We do not usually have to explain to our children that cartoons are not real life or that fairy tales include princesses. As adults, we assume that Hallmark movies will always have similar plots—and that they will likely include tropes such as a small town, a single mom, a handsome widower, and maybe some drama that separates them.

Literary genres are not new. Each book of the Bible falls into a certain genre (or genres), and being aware of this helps us know how to understand what we're reading. In this chapter, we will discuss what it looks like to interpret the genres of law, historical narrative, poetry, wisdom literature, prophecy, Gospels, parables, Epistles, and apocalyptic literature. Each literary genre has its own ground rules for interpretation. It's not always easy—I know I have misinterpreted literary genres more than once. I think the easiest way to misinterpret genre is by taking Bible verses out of their historical and cultural context and trying to apply them to our present-day circumstances. Then, if the promises of these verses do not come true in the way we expect, we get frustrated. When I first learned some of the interpretative elements of genre, I couldn't believe how Scripture came alive for me. I hope the same will be true for you!

Law

The first five books of the Bible (Genesis, Exodus, Leviticus, Numbers, and Deuteronomy) are known as the law books. These books include 613 commands to the Israelites, among which are the Ten Commandments. These books are also called the Pentateuch (meaning "five scrolls") in Christianity and the Torah (meaning "law") in Judaism. It is wise to pay special attention to the first book of the Bible from which all else stems: Genesis. Genesis lays the groundwork for the Bible by detailing the story of Creation and the earliest history of God's people, the Israelites. It is also wise to learn how genre can impact the way we interpret this book. Genesis includes the genres of Hebrew prose, poetry, and historical narrative, along with law. Many of the books of the Bible, although categorized as one genre, are really made up of multiple genres. In Genesis we learn, through the genre of Hebrew prose, that God created a perfect, harmonious garden in which His people would dwell in a relationship with Him: "Then God said, 'Look! I have given you every seed-bearing plant throughout the earth and all the fruit trees for your food. And I have given every green plant as food for all the wild animals, the birds in the sky, and the small animals that scurry along the ground—everything that has life.' And that is what happened. Then God looked over all he had made, and he saw that it was very good!" (Genesis 1:29-31, NLT).

Yet Adam and Eve sinned, rebelling against God's perfect rule. This reality points us toward our need for the law. God later promised that He would bring about a nation through the descendants of Abram (see Genesis 12:1-2). In the book of Exodus, He appoints Moses as a spokesperson for the people of Israel and leads them out of Egypt and into the Promised Land.

To understand the law genre, we must first understand what the law meant to an ancient Israelite. God gave the law to Moses as instruction to His people on how to live in relationship with one another and with God. These laws are often called the Mosaic covenant. (In the Bible, a covenant is a binding promise between God and His people.) The people were commanded to love the Lord their God only, have no other gods, and love others as well (see, for example, Leviticus 19). The law helped them understand how to do that. Throughout the Israelites' journey from captivity to the Promised Land, in the law books we read about the very real ups and downs of the Israelites. Sometimes they loved and were faithful to God alone, but often they were unfaithful to God and broke His laws. Yet God remained faithful to His part of the covenant. The Mosaic covenant was conditional. Both sides had a promise to keep. God gave them the law, and His part of the covenant was if they kept the law, He would bless them; if they disobeyed, He would punish them. In that covenant, God promised to make them a kingdom of priests and a holy nation (see Exodus 19:6). Whenever the Israelites asked for forgiveness and turned back to God, He forgave them and came to save them from their troubles.

God gave the Israelites many different laws, which can be broken down into three categories: moral laws, civil laws, and ritual laws. Every part of God's law showed the people how to live a life faithful to God and loving toward other people.

The first set of moral laws given to the Israelites was called the Ten Commandments. These commandments guided the Israelites to maintain faithfulness to God. God's law helped the Israelites lead upright lives as part of the covenant God made with His people. The moral laws are still applicable today; they have to do with right living and ethics. They show us the heart of God and His desire for our holiness.

Civil laws relate to God's governing of ancient Israel. These laws guided the Israelites, who were God's people in a theocracy (God was King of their nation), on how to treat one another. (See Deuteronomy 24:10-11 for an example of a civil law.) Now, because of Christ, we are in God's Kingdom, and the Spirit of God is within us. These civil laws are not binding for New Testament Christians today, but they help us to understand God's heart for how people can relate to one another when we study these laws.

Ritual laws pertain to sacrifices, cleanliness, and Temple worship. The ritual laws in the Old Testament all pointed ahead to the work of Christ on our behalf. So, for example, the Israelites celebrated the Day of Atonement once a year. On the Day of Atonement, the Israelites had to make sacrifices, release a "scapegoat" into the wilderness, burn incense, and sprinkle blood (see Leviticus 16). All these rituals were intended to purify the Tabernacle and later the Temple and also to cleanse the Israelites from their sins.

Each aspect of these rituals pointed to Christ and His death to cleanse us of our sins. All these ritual laws were fulfilled in Christ's once and for all sacrifice for us. We can now read about these rituals in the Old Testament and learn quite a bit about what Jesus' sacrifice does for us. However, believers are no longer required to perform the rituals because Jesus' sacrifice brings us into fellowship with God (which was the function of the fellowship sacrifice — see Leviticus 7:11-21), and permanently cleanses us from sin and impurity (which the purification offerings did imperfectly—see Hebrews 10:11-14).

Civil and ritual laws are no longer binding on Christians, as the laws find their fulfillment in Christ. Now we know that through faith in Christ we can have a relationship with God; it is no longer through purification offerings that we are cleansed but through what Christ did for us. Now that His Spirit is within us as believers, He guides us on how to truly keep the laws with our whole heart instead of just outwardly performing them. Through the prophet Ezekiel in the Old Testament, God foretold what He would do one day: "I will give you a new heart and put a new spirit in you; I will remove from you your heart of stone and give you a heart of flesh. And I will put my Spirit in you and move you to follow my decrees and be careful to keep my laws" (Ezekiel 36:26-27). The Spirit guides us to have the heart of God as we love others and treat others as Christ would. Unfortunately, the Pharisees show us clearly what it means to live according to the law without the heart of Christ. That kind of righteousness is only outward. Because of what Christ has done, we live from His Spirit in our hearts, and He motivates us to live authentically for Him.

But as Kristie Anyabwile points out, we should not throw away these laws completely or dismiss them as irrelevant. The question then becomes, How do we find an application for these laws within our understanding of their literary genre? Here's how Anyabwile explains it:

> When we look at the content of the law, we will see some recurring themes we should pay attention to, such as God's sovereignty, holiness, and grace; the shape of worship; and how seriously God takes sin. The law shows us that God cares about every aspect of our lives, our bodies, our attitudes toward our family members and neighbors, our celebrations. God is not just handing down random laws to trip up His people. When we read laws about what Israel could eat and what they must refrain from eating, we learn that God is holy and requires His people to live holy lives.[1]

"God is holy and requires His people to live holy lives." That's a big takeaway! The civil and ritual laws were a gift to the ancient Israelites because under the old covenant, it was the only way they could be clean and have a relationship with God. The Israelites had to offer sacrifices to receive atonement for their sins. These blood sacrifices were offered to pay the penalty for their sins and required a priest as their mediator. The consequence for sin is always death, so instead of the person dying for their sin, an animal was killed and its blood was shed.

Though we do not have rules about ritual sacrifices today, the law still applies in this primary way: it reveals to us that we are sinners in need of a Savior. The law still points to a great need within each of us that only Jesus can meet. We know that Christ came to fulfill the law: "Do not think that I have come to abolish the law or the Prophets; I have not come to abol-ish them but to fulfill them" (Matthew 5:17). He became the once and for all sacrifice for our sins (see Hebrews 10:10). We are no longer under the old covenant, where we must make ritual

The law still applies in this primary way: it reveals to us that we are sinners in need of a Savior.

sacrifices for our sins. Under the new covenant, the Spirit leads us and helps us to follow God's heart and to obey Him. We now come to saving faith through our belief in Christ.

> The law reveals our sin and depravity. Even in our best moments we fail to keep the laws of God perfectly. Thus, we must recognize that we need forgiveness and grace. One purpose of the law is to show us our need of God's grace (Rom. 7:7-25). If we stand outside a covenantal relationship with God, it intends to drive us to repentance and to seek God's saving grace. If we stand within that covenantal relationship, it shows us that time and time again we fail to keep the divine stipulations of the covenant and that we must confess our sins (1 John 1:9) and pray, "Forgive us our debts" (Matt. 6:12). . . . We enter into a covenantal relationship with God on the basis of grace alone, and that relationship is maintained on the basis of grace as well.[2]

The Sabbath law is a great example of an Old Testament law that Jesus' death fulfills on the cross in the New Testament. In the Old Testament, we see how God's actions in Genesis and Creation are one of the foundations for Sabbath keeping. After six days of creating, God rested on the seventh day. God told His people to set apart that day, dedicating it to Him. The observance of the Sabbath is also founded on the salvation of the Israelites from slavery in Egypt (see Deuteronomy 5:15). Each week the people would remember how God delivered them. Finally, it was also a sign of the people's covenant with God (see Ezekiel 20:12, 20; Exodus 31:13, 16-17).

This means we now enter into that rest through faith. Sabbath is a pattern set down for us from the Old Testament that I believe we still benefit from participating in, and which I personally still practice. But Jesus is now our ultimate Sabbath rest. He is the once and for all sacrifice that means we no longer need blood sacrifices for our atonement (see Hebrews 10:12-14).

In the Old Testament, the Jews were in covenant relationship with God, but they had to regularly give sacrifices for their sins and keep the requirements of the law. Yet Paul makes it clear in Romans that it just wasn't possible for imperfect humans to fully keep the law because they were still slaves to sin (see Romans 6:17-18). But through faith in Jesus, we are now slaves to righteousness, and the Holy Spirit motivates us and moves us to do what is pleasing to the Lord—not just outward observances, but more importantly, inward heart change and love for God and others.

Hebrews 4 is the passage that talks about Jesus as our Sabbath rest. Through the Cross and our faith in what Jesus did for us through His death and resurrection, we have entered into the Sabbath rest of God.

So if the Sabbath was fulfilled in Christ, why would we practice Sabbath at all? We adhere to Sabbath rest because we *love God* and are thankful for what Christ did on our behalf. I participate in the Sabbath not because I have to but because I *get to* in response to and out of love for my Savior. I participate in the Sabbath because it is a life-giving habit that was patterned for us in the Old Testament and is beneficial for our well-being. It points me toward my limits and reminds me that I am not God. It reminds me again and again that I find my worth in Christ, not in what I do. It urges me to trust God with my finances, time, and purpose.

Ultimate rest is found in Jesus: "Come to me, all who labor and are heavy laden, and I will give you *rest*. Take my yoke upon you, and learn from me, for I am gentle and lowly in heart, and you will find *rest for your souls*. For my yoke is easy, and my burden is light" (Matthew 11:28-30, ESV, emphasis added). But as we know, God's grace does not give us a license to be unruly with our freedom in Christ. There are parts of God's laws in the Old Testament that point us toward truths about the human heart.

The Pharisees did not understand the spirit of the law. They went above and beyond it with their external rule-following mandates, making many rules about the Sabbath—not because their hearts were obedient and loved God but because they were concerned with outward demonstrations of religiosity. The Bible reminds us over and over that we must not ignore people's actual needs in favor of rule-following. On one Sabbath, Jesus let His disciples gather grain to eat on the Sabbath, and on another, He healed a man's hand (see Matthew 12:1-8 and Mark 3:1-6). These activities on the Sabbath show that the Kingdom of God is concerned with the heart, not with external rule-keeping that has nothing to do with our hearts. Practicing Sabbath is still a beneficial spiritual discipline for us today. It can still be a worthwhile practice because it points us toward the truth that we need rest, that we can trust God with our time, and that we often need boundaries to point us toward the reality of our limits! It shows us that we are human, we are not God, and in taking a Sabbath we are actively standing against a culture that promotes striving. Setting aside a day to worship God has blessed my own life. Throughout the genre of law in the Bible, we see that knowing our boundaries and limits is a gift.

God's gift of the law was not for purposeless restriction but for our good. In and through the law, we get to see how obeying God brings about blessing while stepping outside the bounds of His plans always brings heartache and frustration. Through the law, God points us toward His holiness, and that holiness informs our desire to grow more like Him. The law is a gift that reminds us of God's character, and righteousness, and heart for His people.

Historical Narrative

Often, our first introduction to the Bible's historical narratives happens when we are children. Many children are familiar with the Bible stories of characters like Esther, David, Jonah, and Noah. This form of literature—the historical narrative—makes up most of the Bible. Historical narratives make up more than 40 percent of the Old Testament and nearly 60 percent of the New Testament.[3] Some books of the Bible often categorized as historical narratives are Genesis, Exodus, Joshua, Judges, Ruth, 1 and 2 Samuel, 1 and 2 Kings, 1 and 2 Chronicles, Ezra, Nehemiah, and Esther. Storytelling is one of the most ancient forms of communication, and historical narratives are true stories that have been passed down for thousands of years. When you're around a campfire, do your kids ask you to tell stories of when they were younger? Mine do. Or has your husband told you a story for the thousandth time in which the fish gets bigger and bigger? Stories are a powerful way that people connect. I have told my children stories many times to illustrate timeless truths. People get to know one another through stories. First dates begin with stories. New friendships start with stories. One writer says that when we read biblical narratives, we say, "God, tell us your story."[4]

The story of the ancient Israelites is about God—and the story of *your* life is also about God. God works through flawed humans and wrong decisions. God is behind every seemingly insignificant story, bringing about His sovereign will through unlikely events. Every story in the Bible shows God's faithfulness to His people. The historical narrative books depict the overarching storyline of God's relationship with His people: Creation, the Fall, and God choosing to bless Abraham and promising to multiply his descendants. Next, we see God appointing Moses to lead the people and the Exodus from Egypt (see Exodus 1–12) followed by the disobedience of the people and forty years of wandering in the wilderness (see Numbers 32:13). Then, before Moses' death, God announces that if the Israelites follow God they will be blessed, but if they do not obey God, they will be cursed (see Deuteronomy 28). We see Joshua enter the Promised Land with the people and partially conquer it. During the next period, Israel was led by a series of judges, and we read that "in those days there was no king in Israel. Everyone did what was right in his own eyes" (Judges 21:25, ESV). We then enter the period of the kings where God grants the Israelites' desire for a king to rule over them, but most of the kings turn from God and lead the people into evil.

Today, we understand that stories typically include characters and cohesive plots. Hebrew narratives share elements of our modern-day stories, including main characters, supporting characters, riveting plots, a problem, a climax, and a resolution. But Hebrew narratives are also distinct in specific ways: they typically highlight dialogue, focus on characters' decisions, and contain repetition for emphasis. This repetition helps us determine the main themes of the story. Hebrew authors also told their stories with a single very focused plot:

> To give a general overview, every narrative comprises one overall plot. Each plot determines the individual scenes and the arrangement in which they are found. Next,

every scene must have a background (setting), characters, and action (whether physical or verbal). Nothing that is recorded in the narrative occurs incidentally. All the details are there for a reason but must be kept in their proper perspective. Each scene is carefully modulated by the inspired narrator, who has a definite point of view for recording all the events into a historical story and a definite message that is intended.[5]

Historical narrative is part of God's inspired Word—but it's also a story: we need to take note of the plot, the setting, the problem/conflict, and the historical context. It is important to look at the dialogue, and also to see how the different characters either lived in submission to God's will or against it. Although we do not look at these stories as mere lessons in moralism, we still understand that certain characters lived in obedience to God, and others did not. We want to know what God is showing us through the stories.

One significant distinction between Hebrew narratives and Western literature is that Hebrew authors rarely describe people's physical characteristics. Hebrew narratives don't typically detail the physical appearance of a biblical character unless it is essential to the story. For example, when Ehud is described as left-handed in Judges 3:15, that trait is significant to the story's outcome. Similarly, the inclusion of Goliath's stature (see 1 Samuel 17:4) tells us that it's a meaningful detail. Physical descriptions are used sparingly in the Bible, but the ancient authors relied on other types of information when depicting their characters. For example, "Descriptive terms may be based on status (king, widow, wise man, wealthy, old, etc.), profession (prophet, prostitute, shepherd, etc.), gentilic designation (Hittite, Amalekite, etc.)."[6]

Often, we approach a Hebrew narrative and immediately

imagine ourselves as the main character. We identify with David, for example, and envision Goliath as the "giant" in our lives: our temptations, our enemies, or our frustrations. We tell ourselves, *I can slay my giant if I believe!* But this is not the primary way we should approach a Hebrew narrative. There is so much more depth and insight to these historical stories.

When reading a historical narrative, we must try to find the principles in the passage and see how the story brings us to a greater understanding of God's character. For example, in the story of David and Goliath the main principle is that God can be trusted, and that we can have faith that He is with us in the battle. The battle is the Lord's. A principle is "a fundamental truth or proposition that serves as the foundation for a system of belief or behavior or for a chain of reasoning."[7] Hebrew narratives do have moral implications, but they are not there to highlight the main character as much as to show us that God works in and through all the circumstances. As Joe Linares says:

> The plot of historical narrative provides the opportunity
> for important spiritual and moral decisions. Every
> circumstance becomes an occasion to serve God or rebel
> against Him; this is the real crux of the matter. The
> relationship between the external conflict and the spiritual
> conflict is necessary to discern. . . . This should not imply
> that the only significance of historical narrative is in the
> realm of moral choices. Biblical narratives consist of more
> than conflict; they also have progression. This progression
> unveils the Lord's divine purposes through the plane of
> history. . . . Historical narrative is the main supporting
> framework for the totality of God's revelation to man.
> It touches upon almost every kind of theological truth,
> doctrinal issue, attribute of God, and dimension of man.[8]

To gather principles in a historical narrative, we can ask ourselves a few important questions. Don't forget that every book of the Bible can have multiple concerns that it imparts to the reader—it can be multilayered and multifaceted. When trying to perform exegesis—that is, interpret the bigger picture of the passage—it is helpful to know what to look for.

- What are the general truths in this passage? What type of doctrine or transcendent ideal can be taken from this story? How is the story showing me this truth?
- What is the big idea of this passage?
- Does this principle transcend time/culture?
- Is this a theological truth that is confirmed by other passages in Scripture?
- Is the principle about the plain meaning of the story?
- Is the main point of the passage illustrated for me or told to me?
- What does this tell me about the character of God?
- What does this tell me about God's relationship with His people then and now?

When we're looking for the principle or big idea of a passage, let's try to resist the urge to do these things:

- Allegorize the text (find a hidden meaning of the text that's not really there)
- Try to emulate the Bible characters in specific ways that make the way they do certain things out to be a rule or instruction when it is really a story (e.g., fighting others we disagree with by using a slingshot)
- Idealize the Bible characters and try to be like them. As I explained above, Hebrew narratives can teach us morality

and ethical lessons in some sense because each of the characters chooses either to obey God or to disobey Him. But they are illustrated to us; we are not the characters, though we learn and are challenged by the way the characters did life before God. But this is an inside-out application of the text. We are not to just copy the moral attitudes of Bible characters but to submit to the will of God in response to our love for Him and His love for us.

- Set ourselves up as the hero of the story instead of God as the hero.

I often see examples of this last point on social media. I think it is easy to center ourselves in Bible stories, so I want to be gracious in my response here. But I have left many a women's conference feeling like what was elevated was my ability, or my calling, or what I can do for the Lord. Yet is it not such a sweet reminder when what God has done for us is amplified instead? I recently went to a conference where I was encouraged to identify with Deborah (see Judges 4:4). The focus was on all the big things God was going to do through me. Well, that is a great hype-up message, but in the end, I went home to my five babies and my very ordinary life. What I am hinting at here is that we are not Deborah, but we serve the same God she did! He's the same God who empowered, strengthened, and guided her. I can take away many principles from Deborah's life, including how she stewarded her calling in faithfulness. But I can take away even more about who God was to Deborah and who He is to me.

We all want to have a takeaway when we read the historical narratives of the Bible, but it is of utmost importance that we use and apply the Scriptures to grow in our knowledge of the Lord. It is a beautiful thing to be able to read the stories in the Bible and learn from how the characters lived in light of God's direction and rule.

Poetry

I am a very passionate person. I have always expressed myself through the arts. I studied dance as a child and thought that would be my profession, and then I went on to become a writer. The arts have always helped me communicate, and creative outlets feel very satisfying. The genre of poetry in the Bible uses picturesque language to speak of emotional and spiritual truth. Some books of the Bible that contain poetry are Job, Psalms, Proverbs, Ecclesiastes, Song of Solomon, and Lamentations.

Ancient Hebrew poetry is different from much of the Western poetry we are familiar with because it employs parallelism more often than rhyme and rhythm. Parallelism uses repetition and contrast to make a point. In poetry, one must be aware of devices such as wordplay, metaphors, analogies, hyperbole, personification, riddles, and idioms. Poetry appeals to our senses and emotions. It is often more figurative than literal.

A literal approach to Scripture means considering its plain meaning and taking it at face value. A figurative reading means keeping in mind that parts of the text could be symbolic or could represent something abstract.

For example, Psalm 104:2-3 says, "The LORD wraps himself in light as with a garment; he stretches out the heavens like a tent and lays the beams of his upper chambers on their waters. He makes the clouds his chariot and rides on the wings of the wind." These verses beautifully convey God's majesty through literary motifs.

There are so many examples of differing opinions about whether a text is literal or figurative! For example, Jesus told His disciples, "For truly I tell you, if you have faith the size of a mustard seed, you will say to this mountain, 'Move from here to there,' and it will move; and nothing will be impossible for you" (Matthew 17:20, NRSV). Here our faith is compared to a mustard seed. A mustard seed starts off at about one millimeter in diameter, but its plant can grow to be quite large. The emphasis here is actually on the quality of the disciple's faith, not the quantity. You can have a little faith, and God can accomplish so much.

Some readers of Scripture take a more literal approach to this verse, while others view it as more figurative. Those with a literal view think faith-filled believers can literally move mountains (or perform mountain-moving miracles). Those with a figurative view see the mustard seed as representational of how even a little bit of faith can help us surmount big challenges. This last approach aligns more with how Jesus typically uses parables and metaphors in His teachings. Jesus uses metaphors to make a point. We see Him use metaphors and analogies a lot in His teaching because He grants understanding to those who actively engage with His Word and try to understand it.

Often I hear people with good intentions communicate that they take the Bible literally. I believe their concern is to clarify that they do not want to ignore teachings in the Bible or do mental gymnastics to try to avoid obedience. These people are seeking to honor the Lord with obedience. However, understanding that texts are purposefully written as literal or figurative helps us to keep learning, humbly coming to the Bible, and recognizing that we might need to go deeper to understand what the author or speaker is saying.

Parallelism is one of the most critical and important literary forms of Hebrew poetry, and is less common in most of our Western poetry. There are a few different types of parallelism to keep in mind when we're studying the Bible: synonymous, antithetical, climactic, and chiastic.

Synonymous parallelism is the kind of parallelism where the lines repeat the same thought using different words. Here is an example: "Save me, LORD, from lying lips and from deceitful tongues" (Psalm 120:2). You can see in this example how the psalmist repeats the same thought but in different words: "Lying lips" and "deceitful tongues."

Antithetical parallelism means the second line contrasts with the first line. In Proverbs 10:12, you can see the stark contrast between hatred and love: "Hatred stirs up quarrels, but love makes up for all offenses" (NLT).

Climactic parallelism takes a thought, repeats it, and then expands on it or makes it even more pivotal. Psalm 96:7-8 is an example of this structure: "Ascribe to the LORD, all you families of nations, ascribe to the LORD glory and strength. Ascribe to the LORD the glory due his name; bring an offering and come into his courts."

Chiastic parallelism follows an ABBA pattern, starting with one idea (A), then progressing to another idea (B), then repeating idea B and ending with idea A. Here is an example of chiastic parallelism in Proverbs 11:19-20:

A: Truly the righteous attain life,
B: but whoever pursues evil finds death.

B: The LORD detests those whose hearts are perverse,
A: but he delights in those whose ways are blameless.

Poetry is often used in the Bible because it helped an oral society remember what they were learning. When we think about the Psalms in particular, it's helpful to know they were once songs. The Psalms were used in ancient Israel to build communal faith experiences. They were often performed as sacred music among God's people. Knowing the community's songs marked you as a community member. The Psalms can be

The Psalms combine our honest experience with the unchanging nature of our God.

categorized into many different types, including psalms of lament (Psalms 6 and 130); psalms of wisdom (Psalms 1 and 73); psalms of thanksgiving (Psalms 24 and 57); imprecatory psalms, which call on God to judge (Psalms 55 and 69); psalms of praise (Psalm 145); kingship psalms (Psalms 45 and 101); and more.

I love using psalms to pray. They help me to worship God and thank Him for more than my house, clothes, food, and His other provisions. They have helped teach me gratitude for many things.

For example, I love Psalm 107:1-3, which says,

> Give thanks to the LORD, for he is good;
>   his love endures forever.
>
> Let the redeemed of the LORD tell their story—
>   those he redeemed from the hand of the foe,
> those he gathered from the lands,
>   from east and west, from north and south.

This psalm points me toward the spiritual blessings we have in Christ, not just the material blessings. It can be encouraging to take my eyes off my physical blessings and focus on all the blessings that come through my union with Christ. Reading the Psalms has also helped teach me how to express my sorrow through lament.

Here are some of my favorite psalms to reflect on and incorporate into my prayers:

- Psalm 7: "I will give thanks to the LORD because of his righteousness" (verse 17).
- Psalm 34: "I will extol the LORD at all times; his praise will always be on my lips" (verse 1).
- Psalm 138: "I thank you, LORD, with all my heart; I sing praise to you before the gods" (verse 1, GNT).

The Psalms combine our honest experience with the unchanging nature of our God.

Wisdom Literature

The books of the Bible that make up wisdom literature are Job, Proverbs, and Ecclesiastes. Sometimes scholars also include some of the Psalms in this category and parts of the Song of Solomon. Remember what I told you earlier? Books of the Bible can include a mix of genres.

What is wisdom literature? Fee and Stuart define *wisdom* as "the ability to make godly choices in life."[9] Wisdom literature, then, teaches us how to make those godly choices. It includes sayings, poems, and stories that teach us how to live a life of clarity and conviction before the Lord. Wisdom involves seeking God's will in all things, and these books of Scripture provide godly advice and instruction that, when heeded, directly influence a person's life. Godly character leads to godly action, which leads to a fruitful life.

Wisdom literature in the Bible comes in different forms. Some of these forms are stylistic, like poetry; some are concise, like proverbs; and some take the form of discourse, like the book of Job. But in all of them, we are challenged to look at the many uses of symbolic language, imagery, and parallelism to find out what the author intended to say as they urge us toward wise living.

Many of us are familiar with just one type of wisdom literature: the proverb. As defined by Fee and Stuart, proverbial wisdom concerns "practical attitudes and behaviors in everyday life."[10] In Proverbs, we observe the contrast between the wise and the foolish. We often read the book of Proverbs and other wisdom literature like we would a fortune cookie—to our own detriment. When you open a fortune cookie, you may read a Chinese proverb. Recently a fortune cookie I opened up said, "Good news is coming your way." As we read these fortunes, we may laugh, "Oh wow! What does this mean for my future?"

We may read a proverb like "Train up a child in the way he should go; even when he is old he will not depart from it" (Proverbs 22:6, ESV) and we take that simple line as a guarantee for our life and our future. Instead, we should be looking at the proverbs in the Bible as sayings or pieces of advice that point us toward the wise choices and decisions we should make in life. These wise actions often lead to big benefits, but they are not promises.

It's an easy mistake to make. We stake a claim on a verse like Proverbs 22:6 and believe that if we train our children in Christ, they will not depart from the faith. But proverbs are not promises. They offer us wisdom and truth, but in our fallen world, following the proverbs doesn't mean everything will go the way we want. If you train a child in the way they should go, you honor God and make it more likely that your child will stay on a godly path. But I have talked to many godly moms who have seen their children leave the way of righteousness.

Proverbs, of course, have a spiritual element that we do not ascribe to fortune cookies. According to Robert Stein, "They have been formulated not simply by observing 'life,' but by observing life in the light of divine revelation."[11] Take, for example, our often-misinterpreted Proverbs 31 woman. This iconic woman has become an anthem of hope for some Christians yet represents an unattainable goal to many others. But what many people do not realize when studying the Proverbs 31 woman is that she might not be just *one* woman. Many of us reading Proverbs try to imitate her as though she were one exemplary person. But the Proverbs 31 woman is more likely a composite of many exemplary characteristics. Now breathe a sigh of relief because this is not a box you need to fit into! The principles we derive from this passage should encourage us, not make us feel inept. They are observations of a woman pursuing the Lord, yet often they have been turned into a to-do list for the modern mama.

Let's think about some of the characteristics of the Proverbs 31 woman to really dig deeper into the implications of this proverb and how it is characteristic of a total embodiment of wisdom. First, this kind of woman is rare. Toward the beginning of the proverb, we read, "A wife of noble character who can find?" (verse 10). She provides eagerly for her family by working hard. She makes provisions for her family and gives generously to the poor and needy (see verse 20). She is smart; she protects her household and supports her husband. One of my favorite things about the Proverbs 31 woman is that "she can laugh at the days to come" (verse 25). She does not fret because she has complete confidence in God for the future.

The book of Ecclesiastes is another important example of wisdom literature in the Bible. It opens with a narrator who introduces us to the "preacher"—often identified as Solomon. Right away we learn the purpose of much of the book: "The words of the Preacher, the son of David, king in Jerusalem. Vanity of vanities, says the Preacher, vanity of vanities! All is vanity" (1:1-2, ESV).

The preacher tells us that though he pursued knowledge, pleasure, and work, he came to realize that it all lacked meaning. In Ecclesiastes 1:18 the preacher continues, "For with much wisdom comes much sorrow." The more knowledge, the more grief. But the preacher does show us a sharp contrast with life under God. He points us to a greater reality that we can find the purpose of life with God and in obedience to God (see Ecclesiastes 12).

So, how do we interpret these books of wisdom literature? It is important to understand what the author is trying to communicate, and how the shorter points build up to support the main thematic elements of each book. When we read wisdom literature, it is essential to take in the context of the entire book; the points often build on each other. For example, if we were to start in the middle of the book of Job, we might misunderstand the story. Wisdom literature points to wise, righteous living under God's rule. It helps us to grow in discernment and identify the differences between living wisely as the world teaches us and living wisely as God teaches us through His Word. When we read wisdom literature, we should be on the lookout for how God describes those who are proud (see Proverbs 16:18) versus those who fear the Lord (see Proverbs 1:7) and approach God with a teachable spirit. Those who are humble before God (including Job; those who heed instruction in the Proverbs; and Solomon, who says, "The end of a matter is better than its beginning, and patience is better than pride" [Ecclesiastes 7:8]) experience the life-giving gift of wisdom.

Prophecy

The books of prophecy in the Bible are divided into two categories: major and minor prophets. The terms *major* and *minor* refer to length, not significance. There are five major books of prophecy in the Bible: Isaiah, Jeremiah, Lamentations, Ezekiel, and Daniel. There are also twelve minor prophets: Hosea, Joel, Amos, Obadiah, Jonah, Micah, Nahum, Habakkuk, Zephaniah, Haggai, Zechariah, and Malachi. These used to be combined in one large book called "The Twelve." The big elemental theme that runs throughout every book of prophecy is the theme of woes (or curses) and blessings. The prophets are called to speak on behalf of God, urging the people to turn and repent. If they do repent and turn from sin, then blessing will follow. If they choose to continue in sin, there will be grave consequences.

Here is an example of the prophet Isaiah explaining what will happen to those who do not heed God's instruction: there will be consequences. He says,

> Woe to you who add house to house
>> and join field to field
> till no space is left
>> and you live alone in the land.

The LORD Almighty has declared in my hearing:

> "Surely the great houses will become desolate,
>> the fine mansions left without occupants.
> A ten-acre vineyard will produce only a bath of wine;
>> a homer of seed will yield only an ephah of grain."

> Woe to those who rise early in the morning
>> to run after their drinks,
> who stay up late at night
>> till they are inflamed with wine.

ISAIAH 5:8-11

As the Mickelsens say in their book *Understanding Scripture*, "Prophets used drama, song, parable, story, and exhortation. They were used by God to test and refine the people (see Jer 6:27). They proclaimed inevitable judgment as well as judgment that could be avoided if the people changed their ways."[12] The prophets spoke to an unrepentant Israel, warning the people to turn from their ways. Prophets used many different genres to get their message across, but often spoke in the genre of poetry to convey their message.

For example, the prophet Joel explained that the locusts and famine that were happening in Judah foreshadowed a day of judgment, the Day of the Lord (see Joel 2). The Day of the Lord signifies both current events and the final day of judgment when all evil will be eradicated by God. The locusts destroyed all the crops and brought devastation to the nation. Joel warned Judah that if they repented, then there would be blessing, but if they did not, then they would experience God's judgment through enemy armies that would ransack the land like the locust plagues. Here we see Joel pivot from a call to repentance to a focus on God's forgiveness and rich mercy when people obey.

> Then the LORD was jealous for his land
>   and took pity on his people.

> The LORD replied to them:

> "I am sending you grain, new wine and olive oil,
>   enough to satisfy you fully;
> never again will I make you
>   an object of scorn to the nations."
> JOEL 2:18-19

When I first heard of prophecy, I thought it just meant foretelling the future—like a fortune teller with a crystal ball—but I had much to learn on the subject. When I found out that prophecy doesn't just refer to predicting the future, I was rocked by the difference between foretelling and forthtelling. The messages of the Old Testament prophets were typically unwelcome and they were faced with resistance. They proclaimed messages from God to hostile and indifferent audiences. I have often heard it said that prophets were God's mouthpieces. They were speaking on behalf of God in their culture and time period. This is called forthtelling. Forthtelling is speaking into the culture at hand on behalf of God—for instance, speaking about current events and political or religious circumstances. At other times, prophets foretold events in the future that God showed them. Much of the misunderstanding regarding the books of prophecy has come from confusing foretelling with forthtelling. We see both in the books of prophecy: prophecies that do predict the future (foretelling) and also prophecy that speaks into the current happenings in Israel and Judah (forthtelling).

Prophets had a very unwelcome job and typically faced dismissal and threats from the people they were prophesying to. Keep in mind, we must always understand that the prophetic books are God's words, and the prophets were just His chosen mouthpieces. The prophets often called for repentance. Their messages typically announced judgment and drew the people to repentance and right worship. Fee and Stuart explain, "As you read the Prophetic Books, look for this simple pattern: (1) an identification of Israel's sin or of God's love for his people and (2) a prediction of curse or blessing, depending on the circumstance. Most of the time, this is what the prophets are conveying, according to God's inspiration of them."[13] For example, in the book of Joel we see a clear pivot from curses to blessings. The prophet Joel moves from judgment to restoration. He announces blessings for the people of Israel if they repent and pivot their lives away from sin and toward God. He urges them to return to God: "'Even now,'" declares the LORD, 'return to me with all your heart, with fasting and weeping and mourning.' Rend your heart and not your garments. Return to the LORD, your God, for he is gracious and compassionate, slow to anger and abounding in love, and he relents from sending calamity" (Joel 2:12-13).

Prophets were concerned with repentance and holiness. They spoke boldly in the deliverance of their message, with concern for the sinner.

The books of prophecy point us toward our need for holiness

and a God who continually speaks to us about the blessings of right living. I am always amazed at how patient God is with His people. We can apply these books today by learning about God's heart, His graciousness and quickness to forgive, His long-suffering, and His desire for our holiness.

When studying the books of prophecy, we should look for prophecies that have been fulfilled in the past or will be fulfilled in the future. Some prophets point ahead toward Jesus, while others speak of things that were fulfilled long ago. Some prophecies *still* haven't been fulfilled, while others are partially fulfilled. Often commentaries are the best source to help us understand how to interpret the fulfillment of a prophecy.

Gospels

The word *gospel* means "good news." Did you know that sharing good news is linked to joy? In 1994, scientists conducted a study that shows that you actually experience more joy when you share good news about an event than when the event itself happens. "Back in 1994 scientists ran tests to show that when you share good news with others or celebrate the event, you experience additional happiness over and above the happiness associated with the event itself, possibly because in retelling the event, you re-experience it. . . . What's more, the more people you tell, the more your happiness increases."[14]

The Gospels are the books of Matthew, Mark, Luke, and John. Each of these presents us with a different perspective on Jesus' life. The Gospels are unique in that they include many elements of a historical narrative while also containing biographical information about the life, death, and resurrection of Jesus Christ. Yet they are significantly different from modern-day biographies. Instead, they feature many characteristics of Greco-Roman biography.

In the *Dictionary of New Testament Background*, Richard A. Burridge summarizes the case for the Gospels as biography, not a modern-day biography but a Greco-Roman biography:

> Unlike modern biographies, Greco-Roman lives do not cover a person's whole life in chronological sequence, and they have no psychological analysis of the subject's character. As regards content, they may begin with a brief mention of the hero's ancestry, family or city, his birth and an occasional anecdote about his upbringing; usually the narrative moves rapidly on to his public debut later in life. Accounts of generals, politicians or statesmen are more chronologically ordered, recounting their great deeds and virtues, while lives of philosophers, writers or thinkers tend to be more anecdotal, arranged topically around collections of material to display their ideas and teachings. While the author may claim to provide information about his subject (and we note that no ancient lives are written by women), often his underlying aims may include apologetic (to defend the subject's memory against others' attacks), polemic (to attack his rivals) or didactic (to teach his followers about him). Many ancient biographies cover the subject's death in great detail, since here he reveals his true character, gives his definitive teaching or does his greatest deed.[15]

The Gospels were written to four different audiences for four different purposes, but they all have a similar goal in mind: to give an account of Jesus' life and teachings. The Jews had many expectations surrounding the Messiah, the promised Son of David, based on their familiarity with Old Testament prophecies. Many believed that He would rule the Israelites and offer freedom from

Roman oppression. The fulfillment of prophecy underscores the importance of reading the Old and New Testaments in light of each other. For example, each Gospel mentions that Jesus rides a donkey for His triumphant entry into Jerusalem. But we might not understand why the donkey is important unless we are familiar with the prophet Zechariah, who proclaims,

> Rejoice greatly, Daughter Zion!
>   Shout, Daughter Jerusalem!
> See, your king comes to you,
>   righteous and victorious,
> lowly and riding on a donkey,
>   on a colt, the foal of a donkey.
>
> ZECHARIAH 9:9

If we read the book of Zechariah, we realize that Zechariah prophesied about the coming Messiah, and his prophecy is fulfilled in the Gospels. The Gospels intentionally mention the Old Testament prophecies so much because it was important for readers to connect the dots and understand that Jesus is the Messiah.

Each Gospel is organized and purposed to draw out different themes. Matthew, Mark, and Luke are called the synoptic Gospels because they have many similarities. Scholars have sought to compile a narrative of why there are so many literary agreements, similar wordings, and harmonies between the three Gospels and, at other points, differences. The unknown reasoning behind all the similarities is actually called the "synoptic problem." There are many hypotheses as to why they are so similar.

The best way to study these texts is to look at the Gospels side by side. Then we can observe the textual agreements, differences, omissions, and order of the passages. The synoptic Gospels' focus is so similar and yet distinct from the Gospel of John. The synoptic Gospels share many similar stories, including John the Baptist, Jesus' temptation in the wilderness, and His rejection in His hometown.

When we look to interpret the Gospels, we want to do so vertically and horizontally. Interpreting vertically means considering who the author and the audience were, as well as reading the book front to back, all the way through. When we read it vertically, we concentrate on what the author is trying to highlight.[16] For example, John leaves out the birth of Jesus and His childhood and emphasizes Jesus' identity as the Son of God instead.

As we read each Gospel, we need to keep in mind what the author intended for the reader to understand. Each Gospel comes from a different perspective and is intended for a different audience. So who were these Gospels written for?

- Matthew: A Jewish Christian community
- Mark: A Gentile Christian community in Rome that was undergoing persecution
- Luke: Theophilus and Gentile converts
- John: Jews, Gentiles, and Samaritans (everyone)

What did each Gospel emphasize?

- Matthew: Depicts Jesus as King of the Jews
- Mark: Shows Jesus doing the work of God and tells the passion narrative
- Luke: Focuses on Jesus' humanity. Addressed to a more intellectual audience
- John: Shows readers that Jesus is God incarnate

When we read the Gospels horizontally (side by side), we compare the eyewitness accounts of Matthew, Mark, Luke, and John.

For example, all four Gospels mention the feeding of the five thousand and the baptism of Jesus by John the Baptist in the Jordan River. When we look at these four accounts side by side, we take note of any similarities and differences.

In the feeding of the five thousand, we see a principle that comes up over and over again in Scripture: we serve a God who multiplies what we bring Him. Across all four Gospels, we also read of Jesus' baptism, when the Spirit descends on Him like a dove.

Reading the four Gospels side by side makes it easy to take note of the differences in how the authors describe the same event. We can see that each writer expressed the story in different ways. This shows us how important it is for there to be many witnesses, and people who testify of the same events. It encourages me when I seek to share the Good News.

Sometimes it may seem like these differences even contradict each other. But we know the hermeneutical rule that Scripture never contradicts Scripture. So what do we do with these seemingly contradictory passages? First, we must humbly pray that the Lord would reveal the truth of the text to us. Then we can search for a passage of Scripture that deals with our question didactically. (*Didactic* is just a fancy word meaning "meant to teach.") These are the passages of Scripture that explain doctrines and are aimed at *teaching* instead of *storytelling*. So, if we are reading a historical narrative in the Gospels and we are confused by its meaning, we can find another passage in the Bible on the same topic that teaches the moral truth outright. When we are not clear on a specific passage, didactic passages can clear up our uncertainties.

In R. C. Sproul's book *Knowing Scripture*, he says one of his rules is to "interpret the historical narratives by the didactic." This means he generally follows the principle that "the Epistles should interpret the Gospels rather than the Gospels interpret the Epistles."[17] Both hold "equal authority." But the Epistles—or New Testament letters—often help us know how Jesus' words and teachings should inform how Christians and churches act. At the same time, the Gospels show us details of Jesus' life, death, and resurrection that are not found anywhere else. The Gospels may be stories, but they are still theological. They proclaim the Good News of Jesus' death and resurrection and point unbelievers to a saving faith in Christ.

As I've studied the Gospels, I have realized that many threads tie them together. The Gospels all

- describe the life of Jesus;
- contain elements of a historical narrative;
- focus on different aspects of Christ, whether His humanity, deity, or kingship; and
- demonstrate for us the importance of the Cross and the Kingdom.

I realized how beneficial it is to understand the Gospels both vertically and horizontally. Furthermore, when I discovered the similarities between the individual synoptic Gospels, it changed the way I studied them.

The Gospels give us a front-and-center look at Jesus' teaching and His miracles. In and through the Gospels, we observe the historical Jesus, who is also the Son of God.

Parables

Jesus often taught with parables, which are stories that illustrate truths. Many of Jesus' parables include figurative language and imagery that His listeners would have been familiar with, such as sheep, birds, and mustard seeds. These short stories typically illustrate a point or a lesson, often about what life should look like in the Kingdom of God. The everyday examples within parables help listeners learn something of spiritual significance. In the Gospels, many of Jesus' parables include a hidden element that remains unclear to those who do not believe. Sometimes I take a cue from Jesus and communicate truths to my children through stories too. Some of these stories communicate something to my kids that they would not hear if I did not veil it. For example, before the first day of school, I told them about *my* first day of school back in third grade and how a girl in my class was crying. When I saw her crying, I invited her to come sit next to me. I told this story to show my children how to have empathy on a hard day for everyone.

When interpreting a parable, we must remember that it's a story. Then we need to enter the parable through the perspective of the first-century hearers and ask ourselves why Jesus answered their concerns or questions in this way. Lynn Cohick provides a few questions you can ask yourself to dig deep into the meaning of a parable:

> Ask yourself, How would the first-century listeners have understood this? How are the characters developed? For example, are they part of the religious leadership? Are they part of an outsider group, like a tax collector or like a Samaritan? And think through how the first-century listeners would have understood those. Also don't forget to think about the parable in relation to other parables that Jesus gives, or also the way that the Gospel itself is telling the parable. That is, what is the context of the parable in the gospel story itself? In other words, place the parable in the context of the immediate chapter, and even the Gospel itself. Then, ask yourself finally, How

is this parable teaching me about the Kingdom of God?
Is it grabbing at my emotions? Is it causing me to think
differently? How is it affecting me? And then ask yourself,
What is it teaching me about the Kingdom of God?
What does Jesus mean to communicate? What particular
misconception is He fixing?[18]

Epistles

The word *epistle* means letter. There are twenty-one Epistles in
the Bible. They are separated into two categories: Pauline Epistles
and general Epistles. Pauline Epistles are named after their author,
Paul, and are typically addressed to a specific church or group of
people. General Epistles are believed to be addressed to a broader
audience than Paul's letters were. The Epistles sometimes were
written to address specific issues in the church, but sometimes for
other reasons. Galatians and 1 and 2 Corinthians are examples
of letters that were written because of various problems in these
churches. Philippians was written to thank the church of Philippi
for a financial gift and to tell the Philippians about Paul's joy
and encourage them toward godly behavior. Second Timothy
was written to commission Timothy to continue the work Paul
started. Ephesians was written more as a letter of encouragement
and doctrine.

The Epistles follow the general format of a letter. Just like many
of our emails or notes today, the letters often begin with a saluta-
tion and a blessing or prayer for the recipient. They typically end
with a final greeting and farewell.

My mom has made Valentine's Day cards and letters for my
siblings and me since we were kids. As we got older and began to
head to college, sometimes the cards contained pictures or were
designed on the computer, but they always said things she saw in

us and loved about us, along with memories from that year. It is fun to look back at them and remember which situations arose each year, what kinds of challenges were happening in my life at the time, and how I grew. Now I have continued the tradition for my own children! Every year they receive a long Valentine's Day card talking about how much I love them. Similarly, when we read the Epistles, we can also learn about what was happening at the time they were written. Many of them include references to particular occasions, problems, or situations.

But, as in all interpretations, it can be tempting to speculate too much; we might think we know more than we do about the context of an Epistle. Typically, an Epistle was written to a body of believers, although some are written to a specific person like Philemon. When we study these letters, we should seek to reconstruct in our minds the issue that the first-century hearers were coming up against. As Fee and Stuart put it, when seeking to apply a principle from an Epistle, "it must be applied to genuinely comparable situations."[19]

Another general rule for studying an Epistle is that when the first-century hearers and modern hearers share something in common morally or ethically, it will have similar moral meaning in a modern context as it did to the first-century hearers. When a letter does not share "comparable particulars," it will be more challenging to find the application for our lives. Fee and Stuart explain that if the first-century church is not similar in culture and practice to the twenty-first century it can become hard to determine what has direct application for us as modern-day believers. They further explain that the reader must acknowledge when something has "historical particularity"—as in, some of the problems are informed by the specific time in history, specific people being addressed, and specific culture.[20] Our job as readers is to try to determine what principles or directives stand the test of time for the modern-day hearer. A great example of this would be the cultural practice of greeting someone with a kiss. For example, Paul says, "Greet one another with a holy kiss" (2 Corinthians 13:12). There are many cultures today that still greet each other warmly with a kiss on the cheek, but in modern-day America, we might see this as a romantic gesture. This would not be a timeless directive, but one that was stamped by culture. Therefore, this instruction from Paul would not contain comparable particulars with our time period.

When interpreting an Epistle, I find that much of my information can be gathered by understanding the author and audience. When I begin to understand who the author was writing to, I can consult different commentaries on the particular situation that was going on. Then, I can move toward further understanding what timeless truths are being illustrated. But don't forget that we can always glean truths about God's heart for His people through every page of Scripture.

Apocalyptic Literature

Apocalyptic literature can be hard to interpret. It contains a prophetic element and helps us see what is coming. It explains human suffering in light of eternity and focuses on the fact that God will win in the end. Revelation and parts of Daniel are considered apocalyptic. Revelation seeks to uncover or reveal "things that must soon take place" (1:1, ESV). Apocalyptic means an uncovering or a revealing.[21] It is meant to be a divine revelation. There is also a promise in Revelation that it is meant for us to read: "The revelation from Jesus Christ, which God gave him to show his servants" (1:1). The first chapter of Revelation introduces us to the author, John. It was originally written to seven literal churches from the ancient world. These were real churches with real people.

The book of Revelation also assures us that Jesus will come back someday. John takes us on a journey where he details the return of our King: "Behold, He is coming with clouds, and every eye will see Him, even they who pierced Him. And all the tribes of the earth will mourn because of Him. Even so, Amen" (1:7, NKJV).

Apocalyptic literature, such as Daniel and Revelation, is chockfull of imagery and symbolism that can sometimes feel tedious and hard to interpret. The text can feel far-off or otherworldly when it goes on and on about beasts and horns and dragons, oh my!

At the heart of all the mystery and symbolism of Revelation, we see that believers can endure because Jesus reigns and will one day return victorious. In interpreting the books of Revelation and Daniel, we must remember that in Jewish apocalyptic writing, there is a lot of figurative language and anthropomorphisms (human descriptors for God). Mickelsen and Mickelsen point out that "Figurative language is the only way to convey realities that lie beyond human experience."[22] The truth is, we are limited in our understanding and ability to explain many of the images that John and Daniel saw and tried to impart to their readers.

The use of numbers is also very prevalent in apocalyptic literature. For example, "Symbolic use of the number seven comes to much fuller play in the book of Revelation. The book is addressed to seven churches and speaks of seven spirits before God's throne (1:4). We read of seven lampstands (1:12), seven stars (1:16), seven seals (5:1), and more." Why does the number seven have such significance? We cannot be sure, of course, but perhaps "seven appeared significant to ancient people in their then observable cosmos and its order."[23]

Similes—comparisons using the words *as* or *like*—are prevalent in the book of Revelation and other apocalyptic literature. "Revelation is profuse with them. Revelation has so many that the reader needs to think about each one with questions like these:

Why did John feel he should use a simile in this place? How does the simile help us to understand the idea being presented?"[24] When reading apocalyptic literature, do not be afraid to use commentaries. The symbolism we read in apocalyptic literature can feel far off and confusing. Sometimes the symbolism is explained for us in the immediate text or alluded to elsewhere in Scripture (so following cross-references can be helpful), but sometimes we need to grab a trusted commentary to make sense of the vivid imagery.

I have often stayed away from apocalyptic literature out of fear that I will misunderstand it, or because it seems too otherworldly. But one part of the book of Revelation has reminded me time and time again of the blessing that comes from studying apocalyptic literature. Revelation promises that those who read and hear its words will be blessed. It is the only book of the Bible that begins by promising a blessing to all who read it: "Blessed is the one who reads aloud the words of this prophecy, and blessed are those who hear it and take to heart what is written in it, because the time is near" (1:3). So, the next time you feel tentative about reading apocalyptic literature, remind yourself that all of God's words are beneficial to those who hear them. Every part of Scripture serves its purpose in our lives, and it is essential we read all of it.

Why Focus on Genre?

My dad told me once that he went to the eye doctor for glasses—not because he couldn't see, but because he thought glasses were cool. The eye doctor ended up selling him glasses with nonprescription lenses because he begged for them. Can you imagine?

In studying the various literary genres of the Bible, my hope is to provide you with *real* prescription glasses to help you see Scripture clearly. Learning genre completely changed the way I understood the Bible. All of a sudden, I had the words to explain why I was reading a certain passage in a certain way, and I had the words to communicate to others why a certain passage meant what it did. Genre opened my eyes in so many ways, and I am hopeful that you too will find that awareness of genre helps you understand what you are reading more clearly. May an understanding of literary genre make the Bible come to life as you pursue knowing God better. When you're interpreting Scripture, I want you to eagerly take the tools I have given you and try them out. How do these principles lead you to a greater love of God?

Throughout all these genres, we still see the unity of the Bible. We witness the New Testament fulfilling the prophecies of the Old. We see the preeminence of Christ from beginning to end. I used to spend so much time favoring and elevating the humans in Bible stories that I would come away with an observation that had nothing to do with God. Through the study of genre, I have learned so much about applying biblical truths to my everyday life. Pursuing God is a goal that will take us a lifetime. I hope and pray that this information about literary genre serves you well as you chase after Him.

INTERPRET

MY SON POINTED at a road sign we were passing. "What does that sign mean, Mom?"

"It means the lanes merge, honey."

"What does that sign mean, Mom?"

"It means this lane is a right turn only."

"What does that sign mean, Mom?"

My son continued to pepper me with questions about every road sign we observed! I started to get frustrated until I realized I had looked at these signs so many times that I just assumed I knew their meaning, but upon being asked to explain them, I realized there were some I didn't know after all. This can most definitely happen with the Bible. We can be so used to a specific way someone has taught or interpreted a passage in the Bible that we have a hard time understanding it through the lens of the passage's historical and cultural context. We all come to Scripture with preconceived notions that play into our interpretation of certain narratives or passages we are reading. Sometimes letting go of our presuppositions is hard.

To continue the road signs analogy, think of observations as road signs, and interpretations as an explanation of what they mean. We have observed all the road signs in the observation process, and now as we move on to interpretation, we answer the question "What does this mean?" Observation and interpretation are inextricably linked, but there are some critical differences in how to go about pulling out the meaning. As we move on to our next step, we want to find the purpose of what we have just observed. The main point of interpretation is to discover the purpose of the book and passage we are studying. We must make sure that our interpretation aligns with the author's theme or purpose of the book as a whole.

Interpretation Questions

In every book I have ever read on Inductive Bible Study, there is always a word of caution for the reader. Every well-meaning person comes to Bible study with their own presuppositions. Presuppositions are biases or life experiences that might cloud one's analysis of the text. Everyone has them! There is no way around that. But a wise and discerning Bible student is aware that they might come to the text with their own ideas and cultural biases and must be careful not to read these presuppositions into the text.

Let's remind ourselves of the three steps of Inductive Bible Study:

Observation: What do I see?
Interpretation: What does this mean?
Application: How does this apply to me?

Interpretation helps us discover authorial intent and understand the "why" behind every part of Scripture. It shows us the motivation behind the words being written and reminds us to keep the original author and intended audience at the forefront of our minds. Interpretation takes observation a step further by asking why and how. In this section, I will take you through a specific passage of Scripture to illustrate the process of interpretation. Let's look at Ephesians 4:1-2 (NLT) as our example:

Therefore I, a prisoner for serving the Lord, beg you
to lead a life worthy of your calling, for you have been
called by God. Always be humble and gentle. Be patient
with each other, making allowance for each other's faults
because of your love.

Before we dive into interpretation, let's revisit our rules of hermeneutics:

- Scripture interprets Scripture.
- Scripture never contradicts Scripture. (If you think it does, go back and look again.)
- Scripture cannot mean what it did not mean to its original audience.
- Keep the metanarrative in mind the whole time.

- God is the main character of the Bible, not you and me.
- Always, always exercise humility.

Once we have observed the text and ensured we're keeping the rules of hermeneutics in mind, we can move on to our interpretation questions:

- Why did the author include this in the text?
- Why was it written?
- Why did the author say it in this way?
- Why did the original audience need to hear this?
- How is this going to happen?

Why did the author include this in the text?

Answering the question "Why?" helps us to get at the author's intent. For example, when we read Paul's words, we can safely deduce that he wrote them because he wanted to spur the church on to unity, and we might also be able to infer that the Ephesians needed this exhortation for a particular reason! Whenever we read a passage of Scripture, we want to ask, Is the author explaining something, commanding something, exhorting readers to Christian living, or rebuking readers for sinning? Is the author seeking to explain something or teach truth?

Why was it written?

Was it written for a specific purpose? Was it written to describe or illustrate a principle? Was it written to explain something? Was it written to show readers more about God's character? This question can lead us to many insights about the passage. The reason an author includes a teaching can also help us understand the larger context. Does the "why" help us connect a specific teaching to the broader message or point of the passage?

Why did the author say it in this way?

Learning more about the church of Ephesus can give us insight into the reasoning behind why Paul wrote what he did to this group of people. A look at the context of the passage reveals that Paul spent significant time talking about how Jews and Gentiles are now one in Christ (see Ephesians 2:11-22).

Why did the original audience need to hear this?

Can we infer that the audience needed this reminder for a specific reason? When we look at Ephesians 1:1 ("This letter is from Paul. . . . I am writing to God's holy people in Ephesus.") and read the footnote, we learn that some early manuscripts did not include "in Ephesus," which means Paul probably did not intend this letter just for the Ephesians. The letter ended up being circulated to many churches. Unity, humility, and the other qualities listed here are fruit of our union with Christ, and He equips us to love others as He loves us. Displaying these characteristics in love is a sign that we are walking the walk we are called to. We know this is possible because of His grace, but we also know we must extend effort as verse 3 says: "Make every effort to keep the unity of the Spirit through the bond of peace."

How is this going to happen?

Will it come about through God's direct intervention or through His hand at work in human decisions? Is it promised to a specific group of people? Elsewhere in the book of Ephesians, we find that the unity mentioned in the passage comes about by way of the Cross: "His purpose was to create in himself one new humanity out of the two, thus making peace, and in one body to reconcile both of them to God through the cross, by which he put to death their hostility" (Ephesians 2:15-16). We learn here that unity is a gift we receive, and it's only made possible through Christ's death on the cross. But we also know that as believers we have a role in pursuing unity, and we should be "eager to maintain the unity of the Spirit in the bond of peace" (4:3, ESV). Determining how a specific teaching or event unfolds in Scripture helps us to see how God goes about orchestrating His plans. Did God use a certain means to get His message across? Did He use a certain teaching, or certain illustration?

Asking these questions in the interpretation process helps us to discover the main purpose behind the passage, and once we discover the purpose, we can move toward applying it to ourselves. Uncovering the truths of Scripture helps us to know what God was communicating to the original audience—and what He is still communicating to us today.

Word Studies

Word studies are a huge part of understanding what a biblical author is trying to communicate. Word studies involve seeking to define a word in Scripture and discover its original Greek or Hebrew meaning. But sometimes a Bible teacher or expositor can inflate the word's meaning so that it ends up taking over the sentence instead of giving it the appropriate weight. Each word must be carefully examined in its context to help us grasp the full depth of a writer's purpose.

I once attended a women's conference where a teacher spent most of her sermon explaining the meaning of a word from a Bible verse. The problem is she did not know Greek or Hebrew, nor had she consulted someone who understood those languages. She spent too much time on what the word meant in English, the root of the English word, and then explored the Latin origin. By the end of the session, the entire sermon had become about this word that she'd exposited incorrectly. I was so surprised. I know it was probably not her intention to mislead anyone, but it just shows the importance of doing our due diligence and learning how to study the Bible correctly. The whole sermon had little to do with the main purpose of the passage.

When we do a word study, we must understand that each word has a "semantic range," or a range of ways the word in the original language can be translated into English. In her book *Empowered and Equipped*, Julia B. Higgins explains that when participating in a word study, the student of Scripture should seek to do three things:

1. Identify the words for study
2. Discover the semantic range
3. Determine the meaning that fits the context[1]

Once you have considered the semantic range, you can work on determining the meaning that fits the context of the verses you are studying. For instance, think of the English word *sheet*. In the following two sentences, the word has totally different meanings, which are only clear when you consider the context.

1. He slipped on a sheet of ice.
2. I needed a new sheet of paper.

A funny example of misunderstanding a word because of insufficient context comes from my kindergartner, Barkley. The other night, he told me that at school he'd learned about a president who kept running and running and running, and he finally became president after running a *lot* of times. He then proceeded to ask me how many marathons I thought this president had run before he was elected. Barkley misunderstood his teacher, and the word's context wasn't enough for him to grasp the meaning.

For those of us who do not know Greek or Hebrew, I have a few different websites that can be of help. Turn to the appendix on page 239 for more information on these word study resources.

Introductions

Introductions and conclusions can be acknowledged in the observation phase, but when seeking to answer the deeper question of purpose, I find that introductions and conclusions provide an invaluable step in discovering the "why" of a text, as well as its significance. We often skip over introductions and greetings when studying the Bible, but typically, a book's introduction can give us a window into what the book is about, who wrote it, and who the audience was. Introductions are the opening lines that start any book of the Bible. In the Epistles, this is usually where the author introduces himself or greets the audience. We are all familiar with introductions in our own lives. When we meet someone new, we typically choose a few words to say about ourselves—where we live, what we do for work, and more. This was not how Paul introduced himself. He was not concerned with what he did—he was concerned with whom he served.

If you look up the first few verses of each of Paul's letters, you will find a different way that he describes himself. In Romans, he introduces himself as "a slave of Christ Jesus" (1:1, NLT). Here are a few other examples:

"From Paul, a slave of Christ Jesus, called to be an apostle, set apart for the gospel of God" (Romans 1:1, NET).

"Paul, called to be an apostle of Christ Jesus by the will of God, and our brother Sosthenes, To the church of God in Corinth, to those sanctified in Christ Jesus and called to be his holy people, together with all those everywhere who call on the name of our Lord Jesus Christ—their Lord and ours" (1 Corinthians 1:1-2).

"This letter is from Paul and Timothy, slaves of Christ Jesus. I am writing to all of God's holy people in Philippi who belong to Christ Jesus, including the church leaders and deacons. May God our Father and the Lord Jesus Christ give you grace and peace" (Philippians 1:1-2, NLT).

"This letter is from Paul, chosen by the will of God to be an apostle of Christ Jesus, and from our brother Timothy. We are writing to God's holy people in the city of Colosse, who are faithful brothers and sisters in Christ. May God our Father give you grace and peace" (Colossians 1:1-2, NLT).

Sometimes the purpose or a theme of the book might be clearly stated at the beginning of the book or in the conclusion (which we'll look at next). Therefore, a diligent student of the Word should always look at the "bookends" of the book they're reading, both to discern the purpose and to understand the "why" behind the text.

And this doesn't apply only to the Epistles. Genesis 1:1-2 says, "In the beginning God created the heavens and the earth. Now the earth was formless and empty, darkness was over the surface of the deep, and the Spirit of God was hovering over the waters." In Greek, *genesis* means "in the beginning." This introduction to Genesis tells us what the book of Genesis is about: the beginning of creation!

Another example can be found in the book of Ruth. In the introduction, the author sets up the scene and gives us very important information about the setting of the book: "In the days when the judges ruled, there was a famine in the land. So a man from Bethlehem in Judah, together with his wife and two sons, went to live for a while in the country of Moab" (1:1). Right then and there you get an introduction to the setting, the historical and cultural context, and some of the characters in the story!

Conclusions

Similarly, a conclusion often provides a valuable takeaway. The book of Ecclesiastes sums up its message in the final chapter: "That's the whole story. Here now is my final conclusion: Fear God and obey his commands, for this is everyone's duty. God will judge us for everything we do, including every secret thing, whether good or bad" (12:13-14, NLT). The book of Job ends this way: "After this, Job lived a hundred and forty years; he saw his children and their children to the fourth generation. And so Job died, an old man and full of years" (42:16-17).

As we discussed earlier, it is important to take note of connecting words. Some connecting words are categorized as "terms of conclusion." They indicate the summing up of a thought or purpose. Some words of conclusion include *therefore, thus, and so,* and *for this reason.*

Something to consider: always pay close attention to what comes after these terms of conclusion. It's bound to be important!

Cross-References

Cross-references are the small notations in your Bible that appear at the bottom or center of the page and direct you to other biblical texts. In simple terms, following cross-references helps you see how all the books of the Bible are woven together. When following a cross-reference, you acknowledge that other passages of Scripture can shine light on what you are reading. This is one way to apply the hermeneutical principle that Scripture interprets Scripture.

In the Gospels, we see that Jesus quotes Scripture often. But did you know He uses an ancient teaching method called *remez*? *Remez* means "hint."

Rabbis in Jesus' day would often use this technique when they taught. A rabbi would allude to a particular portion of Scripture from the Old Testament, and his audience would understand what he was saying because they knew the context of the Old Testament passage. Because the Jews were so familiar with the Old Testament, when Jesus quoted Scripture, the context immediately came to mind. Much of the meaning of Jesus' teachings is lost on modern-day readers because we are unfamiliar with the Old Testament.

An example of *remez* would be me saying, "Our Father in heaven, hallowed be your name, your kingdom come, your will be done" (Matthew 6:9-10). You would know I was referring to the Lord's Prayer. Similarly, when Jesus taught, His audience knew the implications of the Old Testament passages He used.

In Luke 4:18-19, Jesus quotes from Isaiah 61: "The Spirit of the Lord is on me, because he has anointed me to proclaim good news to the poor. He has sent me to proclaim freedom for the prisoners and recovery of sight for the blind, to set the oppressed free, to proclaim the year of the Lord's favor." When Jesus' original listeners heard Him quote from this passage, they knew He was alluding to an Old Testament prophecy about the Messiah—the anointed One sent from God—and claiming to be the fulfillment of that prophecy. This was a big claim.

Luke tells us how the people eventually responded to Jesus' *remez*: "They got up, drove him out of the town, and took him to the brow of the hill on which the town was built, in order to throw him off the cliff" (Luke 4:29). Now you understand why they wanted to kill Him. They realized He was claiming to be the long-awaited Messiah, and He was claiming that Gentiles would receive God's favor instead of the Israelites! He even refers to the Old Testament when He talks about Elijah and the widow of Zarephath (see verse 26), further illustrating God's inclusion of Gentiles in the Kingdom of God.

In this passage and many others, cross-references help us to see how the story we're reading interweaves and intersects with passages and stories elsewhere in the Bible.

Commentaries

On a packed train to Austria when I was around ten years old, my dad was robbed. Out of instinct, he felt his back pocket and realized someone had swiped his wallet. He began to yell, "Someone took my wallet!" He was frantic.

Everyone around him began to scramble, looking around for the culprit. The thief must've known he was about to be found out because he dropped the wallet, and people began to point at the floor. "There, there!" they shouted in unison. The train was full in every direction we could see, but all eyes and arms pointed in the same direction. My dad shuffled forward and grasped his wallet.

When I find myself struggling to determine the meaning of a text, I pick up a few trusted commentaries to see which way they are pointing.

The consensus of fingers pointing in the same direction is one way I like to picture the many biblical commentaries we have access to. When I find myself struggling to determine the meaning of a text, I pick up a few trusted commentaries to see which way they are pointing. Often, I am excited to learn that I interpreted a biblical passage accurately. Other times, I am discouraged to see that my own cultural biases have gotten in the way of my interpretation. It is humbling to know that we all come to the pages of Scripture with preconceived notions and perspectives. That's one reason I am thankful to have so many biblical scholars who keep me within the bounds of solid biblical understanding.

Commentaries also help us as we seek to understand the historical, cultural, and political settings of the Bible. When you know that Beethoven became deaf around the age of forty-four, it brings so much more awe to his musical compositions. Similarly, knowing about the bitter hatred between Jews and Samaritans helps the story of Jesus and the Samaritan woman at the well (see John 4:1-42) come alive. According to the book *Understanding Scripture*, "The Samaritan woman with whom Jesus talked at the well of Sychar came from a history of 500 years of political conflict with the Jews. This history of antagonism colored her feelings. Her remarks and the statement, 'Now Jews do not associate on friendly terms with Samaritans' (author's translation) in John 4:9 show that animosity was the accepted way of life."[2]

Jews in Jesus' day wouldn't even travel through Samaria—they hated the Samaritans that much. But John 4:4 tells us that Jesus *did* go through Samaria. Jesus had a purposeful appointment with this woman. The historical context also gives meaning to the Samaritan woman's surprise when Jesus approaches her: "The woman was surprised, for Jews refuse to have anything to do with Samaritans. She said to Jesus, 'You are a Jew, and I am a Samaritan woman. Why are you asking me for a drink?'" (John 4:9, NLT). Knowing the cultural and political background of this passage helps us understand its significance. Reading commentaries gives us a scholarly perspective on various kinds of insights, including what the original Greek or Hebrew words mean and various historical facts that could affect our interpretation of the passage.

Explicit versus Implicit Themes

When we look at Scripture, it's a good idea to ask, "What are the predominant themes throughout the pages? What are the obvious and less obvious themes?" The main goal of interpretation is discovering the purpose of the text, and identifying themes is an important element of that. A theme is the main idea, or purpose of a passage.

If it helps, you can summarize each theme of the section you are studying in one sentence. Writing out exactly what you discover helps you move closer to discovering the purpose behind the words. Themes are often found by highlighting key words and repeated words. Then you can look further into themes by determining whether or not a purpose statement has been included in the introduction or conclusion. You can also discover themes by looking at ideas that seem to be developing or progressing through the pages of Scripture. Do you see an idea that the Bible mentions over and over (for example, a garden, a seed, the tree of life)? Follow the theme like breadcrumbs to see where it leads.

I recommend highlighting themes in your Bible by simply drawing a large parenthesis next to the paragraph and writing down exactly what you believe the theme to be, which can then point you toward the main point or overall purpose of the passage after you have completed all the other steps of interpretation. You could also use a journal or sticky notes to mark these alongside the other notes in your Bible. Another beneficial way to study is to print out a book of the Bible with large margins and spacing, and mark it up, highlight, and write all over it to your heart's delight.

The books of the Bible often impart multiple themes to the reader. These themes are multilayered and multifaceted, and we would do well to perk up, pay attention, and try to identify them.

Typology and Promises

My sister-in-law once told me that she dressed her five kids in lime green whenever she took them to busy places. When we were playing at the playground one day, they all were wearing these bright matching shirts, and my eyes kept being drawn to them. I am sure certain things jump out at you from the pages when you are studying the Bible. Your eyes become trained to see certain things. Just like our eyes see key words, themes, or genres—or even settle on certain ideas over and over again—we can find that we begin to see typology and promises throughout the pages of Scripture.

Typology refers to events or people in the Old Testament that point ahead to Christ or another key element of the New Testament. Promises are pledges about future fulfillment. When God promises something to His people, He is always faithful to keep that promise.

Typology

We need to know how to identify typology in order to understand the Old Testament. Typology alludes to the coming of Christ and anticipates God's future plan of redemption. Typology can be present in all sorts of genres. It can take the form of promises or be found in certain events or people, such as Old Testament characters like David who foreshadow Christ (see Revelation 22:16). David's life points to Christ throughout Scripture. When he defeats Goliath, he foreshadows Jesus' defeat of Satan. As a shepherd, he foreshadows the great Shepherd. And when he is a king, he helps us anticipate the King of kings. In the book of Genesis, there are many instances of typology. When you read through Genesis, I urge you to write down any promises made to the Israelites or mentions of the patriarchs. Ask yourself how these might point to God's plan of redemption and the coming of Christ. In Genesis there is quite a bit of foreshadowing of Christ through Adam, Joseph, and Melchizedek.

Promises

Promises can be defined as purposeful statements from God that show us that He is a God who keeps His word and is faithful to His character. These promises are a big part of God's overall plan of redemption.

In Genesis, we want to pay careful attention to the Creation account and be on the lookout for two specific things, according to James E. Smith: patriarchs and promises. "Genesis can be summed up in the words *patriarchs* and *promises*. The book focuses on the fathers of the Israelite nation and the promises that God made to them."[3] In the books of Genesis through Joshua, we see the Abrahamic promise. The Lord said to Abraham, "I will make you into a great nation, and I will bless you; I will make your name great, and you will be a blessing. I will bless those who bless you, and whoever curses you I will curse; and all peoples on earth will be blessed through you" (Genesis 12:2-3).

The promise shows us that God's blessing on Abraham results in a nation that will be a blessing to the whole world, which is ultimately fulfilled in the coming of Jesus Christ. This promise of blessings sets the stage for the law given to Moses all the way to Joshua entering the Promised Land.

From 1 Samuel to 2 Chronicles, we see the Davidic promise, which shows us God's intention to use David's lineage as Christ's lineage. We read the Davidic promise in 2 Samuel chapter seven. Through the prophet Nathan, the Lord promises to establish a kingdom through David's son Solomon, but He goes on to promise an eternal Kingdom through David's descendant, saying, "Your house and your kingdom will endure forever before me; your throne will be established forever" (2 Samuel 7:16). This eternal Kingdom is fulfilled in Christ.

It can be easy to misinterpret or misunderstand promises in the Bible, especially if we take them out of context. Here are two questions I always ask myself when I come across a promise in Scripture:

- Was this promise given to a specific audience at a particular time in history?
- Is this promise conditional or unconditional?

The first common mistake is interpreting a portion of Scripture as a promise for us when it was intended to be for a specific audience at a specific time in history. The danger of claiming a biblical promise not meant for us is that we can become disillusioned or confused if we apply it to ourselves and don't see it fulfilled. For example, God told Abraham that He would give land to him and his offspring (see Genesis 13:14-17). If you interpreted this as a promise to you, then you would be disappointed if God didn't provide you with land. That is a silly example, but it's easy to make a similar mistake with promises such as Jeremiah 29:11, as I explain later in this section.

I love being a middle child. I had an older sister and a younger brother, and I was the stereotypical middle child. I loved being friends with either side of the family, but I was always scheming and looking for attention from everyone. I have a vivid memory of taking full advantage of my eldership. One year, I had a great idea: I convinced my younger brother that he should trade his larger bedroom for my smaller bedroom and that I would "throw in the playroom." Therefore, he would be getting two for the price of one. The problem with this deal was that I did not own the playroom. It was basically a family room, yet I had tricked him into believing he could hold the playroom as his own. He willingly agreed because this seemed like a win-win situation. He got two rooms, while I was left with the oversized bedroom. I still feel bad for the lack of parental supervision and his willingness to appease his big sister. He quickly realized that he'd laid claim to a room that was not actually his. We can do the same with biblical promises without meaning to. There are so many beautiful promises in Scripture we can lay claim to like "I will never leave you nor forsake you" (Hebrews 13:5, ESV), and there are some that, based on context, were written to a specific group of people at a particular time in history. Many misinterpret promises in the Bible by not considering context and who the promise was for. Was it to a general audience or to the body of believers (meaning it's also a promise to you and me), or was it to the Israelites at a particular time in history on a specific occasion?

One example of a commonly misinterpreted promise is Jeremiah 29:11: "'I know the plans I have for you,' declares the LORD, 'plans to prosper you and not to harm you, plans to give you hope and a future.'" Jeremiah is mostly a book of prophecy, but it also has historical narrative woven throughout. This verse was a promise from God to the nation of Israel, communicated through the prophet Jeremiah. It is familiar to most people as a promise written on mugs, greeting cards, and T-shirts. It seems to be every college graduate's motto as they leave their campus and venture out into the great unknown. It is often taken out of context to mean that God has a plan for deliverance and prosperity for me today in whatever situation I am facing. But when we read this verse in the context of Jeremiah's book, we see that God isn't promising immediate deliverance but instead promising hope to the Israelites when they were in exile experiencing hardship. It isn't a verse directed at me; it's a verse to a collective group of people, the Israelites.

This verse was given to a specific group of people during a particular time in history. It can still encourage our hearts, but not because we proclaim it as a personal promise. Instead it shows us God's character. He was faithful to Israel; He will be loyal to us even amid suffering, heartache, and turmoil. Although life might be full of pain, we know that God gives us hope during times of trial. All of Scripture gives us insight into who God is and how He loves and cares for His children, and in faith we can ask Him to love and care for us in our situations as well. Claiming what God will *do* for us and proclaiming who God *is* for us are very different attitudes coming from studying these kinds of promises. Understanding who God is for us is always a proper application when it comes to a promise.

Before we claim a promise from Scripture, we must ask ourselves whether it is ours to claim. The Bible contains many beautiful promises from God, and we can claim many of them for ourselves. They give us comfort in uncertain times and help us to understand God's heart. Promises can be a beautiful anchor for us in uncertain times.

Another common mistake is misunderstanding a conditional promise for an unconditional one. A conditional promise requires us to live in the manner that God desires us to live, while an unconditional promise is not dependent on us or our actions. Many of God's promises are conditional on us living in the way that God knows is best for us. Psalm 37:4 says, "Delight yourself in the LORD, and he will give you the desires of your heart" (ESV). He will give you the desires of your heart, but first you must delight yourself in the Lord. "Therefore submit to God. Resist the devil, and he will flee from you" (James 4:7, NKJV). The devil will flee from you, but first you must submit to God. "Blessed is the one who perseveres under trial because, having stood the test, that person will receive the crown of life that the

Lord has promised to those who love him" (James 1:12). Once a person perseveres and has stood the test, that person will receive the crown of life.

An example of an unconditional promise throughout Scripture is "Do not fear, for I am with you; do not anxiously look about you, for I am your God. I will strengthen you, surely I will help you, surely I will uphold you with My righteous right hand" (Isaiah 41:10, NASB). This is a perfect example of a promise that applies to us no matter what. We might undergo trials, but God promises to strengthen us.

We have talked a lot in this section about things not to do, but we should equally consider what *to* do! There are so many beautiful Bible verses that we can lay claim to. The Bible is meant to provide comfort to us in seasons of distress. Here are some of my favorite promises that can be found in Scripture.

- "My message and my preaching were not with wise and persuasive words, but with a demonstration of the Spirit's power, so that your faith might not rest on human wisdom, but on God's power" (1 Corinthians 2:4-5).
- "Those who hope in the LORD will renew their strength. They will soar on wings like eagles; they will run and not grow weary, they will walk and not be faint" (Isaiah 40:31).
- "Let us hold unswervingly to the hope we profess, for he who promised is faithful" (Hebrews 10:23).
- "God opposes the proud but gives grace to the humble. Humble yourselves, therefore, under the mighty hand of God so that at the proper time he may exalt you, casting all your anxieties on him, because he cares for you" (1 Peter 5:5-7, ESV).
- "You will keep in perfect peace those whose minds are steadfast, because they trust in you" (Isaiah 26:3).

A Spectacular View

When I was a kid, my parents' best friends were missionaries in Nepal. They invited us to go with their family on a weeklong adventure hiking in the Himalayas. Nepal was one of the most interesting countries I had ever been to! The markets, the smells, the pungi-playing snake charmers. Sherpas helped us navigate the mountains—they knew the terrain like the back of their hands. I still remember getting to drink yak's milk as a warm and cozy version of hot chocolate at one of the rest stops! We would hike all day and crash at night at different lodges along the way. The lodges were bare and

In seeking to interpret Scripture more accurately, you are climbing the steps one by one.

rustic, but provided some of the best memories of my childhood. My sister and I would stay up late, talking into the night until we woke up again to hike to the next spot. I will remember some of those sights forever—they were breathtaking. One particularly memorable spot was a valley with what seemed like millions of little steps. Once we climbed all the steps, we had an aerial view of the landscape for miles around. The climbs were hard, but the views made it all worth it. (I was young and had endless amounts of energy to summit the mountain cliffs and get to the points with all the views!) In seeking to interpret Scripture more accurately, you are climbing the steps one by one. It can be difficult, and you might want to give up, but at the end you will be rewarded with a spectacular view of the ancient landscape of the passage you are studying. What a gift to then move on to seeing how this life-changing perspective impacts your walk for the rest of your life.

12

APPLY

SECRET CONFESSION: I drove a minivan in college. Other students called me "soccer mom." Then, like a prophecy fulfilled, I married and had five kids. The reality was that my missionary parents had loaned me their white minivan while they were overseas. Rather than being embarrassed, I remember being so excited to have that vehicle to drive my friends around. Being a spontaneous soul, I regularly took spur-of-the-moment trips to Chicago to visit my sister. I once told friends to jump in to go get "cheesecake factory." Three hours later, we arrived at The Cheesecake Factory! Without any redeemable goal or aim beyond spontaneity in life, we drove into Chicago, ate cheesecake, wasted the rest of the night driving around, and finally parked to sleep. Wow, those were the days when I had so much time on my hands.

Today? I would never drive anywhere without a good reason

to do so. Let me speak that a bit louder. I WOULD NEVER go somewhere for no reason because I know there would be unwilling hostages in the back (aka children), buckled tight, unhappy, and wanting to get to their destination as quickly as possible. I remember on one of those spontaneous college trips I got pulled over by the police for rolling through a stop sign. Instead of yielding and coming to a complete stop, I rolled right through the intersection. I was fortunate—I got off easy with a stern warning. Road signs are there for a reason. They serve an important purpose in keeping everyone safe because they tell us how to behave. The Scriptures are intentional road signs to abundant life, not spontaneous car trips without meaning or purpose.

We've already talked about how, when we study Scripture, first we observe the road signs, then we learn what they mean, and finally we make a decision to either heed them or not. It's that simple. For most of us, it comes naturally to read the Bible and apply it to our own lives—so much so that often we miss the other two crucial steps of observation and interpretation. And, as I love to remind the students I teach, *the Bible is meant to be applied.* We do want the Bible to change our lives, but if we want that to happen, we cannot just skip the process of how we get there. There's no clicking our heels like Dorothy to bypass the process and arrive back home in Kansas. Application is where we begin to transport ourselves from observing the strange biblical land of Oz to learning how the Bible applies to us here at home.

For example, we cannot find out what the message of Scripture really means if we have not done the hard work of finding out what it meant to a first-century Jew. Once we have discovered what it meant to the original audience, we then have building blocks for our application. Every road sign has a purpose behind it. Every verse of Scripture has a purpose behind it. We all know that the red octagonal road sign screams *STOP*. It is not placed there to inconvenience us, but rather for the safety of ourselves and our passengers. The Scriptures, like those road signs, provide the guidelines we need for our journey on earth.

The Final Step

In this chapter, we are going to talk about the final step in the Inductive Bible Study process: application. This is when we take what we've observed and interpreted in the Scriptures and ask, "How does this apply to me?" or "What can I learn about God's character from this passage?" In keeping with the road sign analogy, "What do I do with this stop sign before me? Apply the brakes? Or ignore the sign to my and others' peril?" For what good is a sign if we do not *do* what it says? We want to make sure in the application process that we are also taking the time to learn about God through the pages of Scripture. You might be thinking, *Duh!*, but often our takeaways can just be about ourselves and we can forget that reading Scripture is intended to lead to a richer understanding of who God is. Scripture is meant to build our relationship with God and to show us who He created us to be.

As a general rule, I begin with the two simple principles of application laid out by Fuhr and Köstenberger. The first question to answer about the passage we're studying is whether it is a "knowing" or a "doing" text. They write,

> In many biblical texts, the author sought to instruct and inform his reader concerning God, humanity, or some aspect of God's redemptive plan for humanity. In these texts, the author wanted his original audience to receive knowledge—an element of truth to be appropriated by the mind more so than practiced through tangible activity. In other cases, the primary thrust was action based—the

original author wanted the original recipients of the text to do something. Therefore, as we work through the process of determining legitimate application, it's helpful to discern whether the primary thrust of application for the original audience pertained to knowing something or doing something. Legitimate application in our day will typically follow suit.[1]

Depending on whether we're studying a knowing or a doing text, we will find encouragement to either change our mind or our behavior. Bridging the gap between interpretation and application becomes easier when we are clear on what the theme, purpose, or principle is.

At this point, you have learned to observe and interpret the road signs of Scripture, and now it is time to decide whether you will heed them or not. What we decide speaks to what we believe. Let me give an example of an application of Scripture based on knowledge we have attained. Consider the story of the Last Supper. There we find all twelve disciples sharing an intimate meal with Jesus. Suddenly Jesus announces the disturbing fact that there is one among His disciples who will betray Him. All the disciples, except one, ask Jesus, "Am I the one, Lord?" (Matthew 26:22, NLT). But there is one disciple, Judas, who adjusts the question. "Judas, the one who would betray him, also asked, 'Rabbi, am I the one?' And Jesus told him, 'You have said it'" (Matthew 26:25, NLT).

Did you notice the difference in address? While all the disciples now recognized and believed that Jesus was their Lord and addressed Him as so, Judas showed his belief about Jesus by calling Him Rabbi (teacher) instead of Lord. This is a slight but eternally significant difference. There's truth here that we don't want to miss. We can believe Jesus is a good teacher, we can learn valuable principles from Scripture, and we can do those things without ever surrendering our lives to Him as Lord. Jesus *is* a good teacher, but at some point we have a decision to make. Do we believe that Jesus is just a teacher to us, or are we ready to surrender to Him as Lord? And let's not forget that even calling Him Lord is not enough if we do not demonstrate that belief by submitting to His Word.

This is a good example of application based on "knowledge attained." When we understand that the knowledge we have attained from our study brings us understanding of the distinction between the words *Rabbi* and *Lord*, then we can apply it. We can see and understand that we must do more than just think Jesus is a good teacher—we must believe in Him as our personal Savior (see Ephesians 2:8-9).

Doers of the Word

I'm sure we can all agree that we can be hearers of God's Word while not being doers. But submitting to the application part of Scripture study means we internalize it and do what it says. Consider this famous passage in the book of James: "What good is it, my brothers and sisters, if someone claims to have faith but has no deeds? Can such faith save them? Suppose a brother or a sister is without clothes and daily food. If one of you says to them, 'Go in peace; keep warm and well fed,' but does nothing about their physical needs, what good is it? In the same way, faith by itself, if it is not accompanied by action, is dead. But someone will say, 'You have faith; I have deeds.' Show me your faith without deeds, and I will show you my faith by my deeds. You believe that there is one God. Good! Even the demons believe that—and shudder" (2:14-19).

As James suggests, if we have faith but don't apply it, then is the Word of God penetrating our hearts and changing our minds? Or have we merely become hearers of the Word and not doers?

Being a doer of the Word means we are concerned that our talk matches our walk, that our Christlikeness is evident by how we follow the Spirit, listening to His promptings when He moves us to change. We do this by reading God's Word and applying it to our lives. The Spirit speaks through the pages of Scripture. Ephesians 4:22-24 sums it up so well: "Put off your old self, which belongs to your former manner of life and is corrupt through deceitful desires, and . . . be renewed in the spirit of your minds, and . . . put on the new self, created after the likeness of God in true righteousness and holiness" (ESV). Putting the old life off and the new life on happens through regeneration, which is only possible through Christ's work on our behalf. We can't do it ourselves. But we are called to walk in this new life as doers of the Word, and that means our lives are going to look different from the world.

We were recently in Florida, and my sons searched for geckos the whole time! Growing up in Thailand and vacationing in Florida, I have seen many geckos and am often reminded of this principle of putting off our old lives and putting on the new. God created geckos with an amazing feature. If a gecko becomes fearful or gets caught by a predator, it is able to simply detach from its tail and run off. Isn't that cool? This made for some tailless geckos around our house. Eventually, new tails grow back—but they do not look like the old tails. Like geckos lose their tails, we are called to put off our old natures. As we grow spiritually, we will grow in new ways that will not look like the old but will be evidence of God at work in our lives. We will no longer look like the world because our speech, morals, and the way we work will all be done unto the Lord.

During the application process, we can ask a myriad of questions, such as these:

- Is this an area of submission or obedience that God is asking me to grow in?
- Why does what God says matter here? And how should I respond?
- Is God asking me to change a habit or rethink a belief?
- How can I let this word of comfort encourage my heart?
- How does this impact my understanding of God?

Everything we read in the Bible is meant to transform us, sanctify us, and help us grow into Christlikeness. Every word is purposeful, so we must be prayerful in the application process to listen to the Holy Spirit's encouragement, conviction, and guidance. We must hold the Scriptures before us prayerfully and ask the Lord what He is teaching us.

We all long for intimacy with God. In the same way that a special song moves you and may even lead you to dance, the pages of Scripture are those notes that sing out what it looks like to dance with God. We are not solo performers but intricately connected to God through the dynamic pages of Scripture (see Hebrews 4:12). Does that not excite you? As we encounter God through His Word, we also grow in intimacy with Him.

We are not solo performers but intricately connected to God through the dynamic pages of Scripture.

Loving God and Others

I like to think about the application of Scripture in two different ways: my relationship with God and my relationship with others.

The biblical basis for this is found in Matthew 22:37-40. Jesus says, "'Love the Lord your God with all your heart and with all your soul and with all your mind.' This is the first and greatest commandment. And the second is like it: 'Love your neighbor as yourself.' All the Law and the Prophets hang on these two commandments." There we have it, application of Scripture impacts our relationship with God and our relationship with others.

In our relationship with God, the application of Scripture may challenge us and may bring to light or emphasize questions such as these:

- Am I loving God by placing Him above all else? If I place Him first, what impact will that have on me? On my life? On my family?
- How has what I'm learning taught me more about what God's character is like? For example, how has He revealed His faithfulness to me? Has this grown my faith? Has it led me to reverent worship? Has it exposed sin within me, leading me to repent and ask for forgiveness?

Or in our relationship with others, the application of Scripture may also challenge us and bring to light or emphasize questions such as these:

- In what way does this Scripture spur me on to love others like Christ does?
- Is God asking me to respond differently than I have been toward others? For example, do I need to adopt more of a servant's heart (see 1 Corinthians 4:1-2)? To avoid strife or jealousy (see 1 Corinthians 3:3)? Or to get control of my tongue (see James 1:26)?

If we let it—if we apply it—Scripture will have a powerful impact on our love for God and others. As Ephesians 4:15 says, "Speaking the truth in love, we are to grow up in all aspects into Him who is the head, even Christ" (NASB). Or as Colossians 1:9-10 says in this wonderful prayer, "We ask God to give you complete knowledge of his will and to give you spiritual wisdom and understanding. Then the way you live will always honor and please the Lord, and your lives will produce every kind of good fruit. All the while, you will grow as you learn to know God better and better" (NLT).

Growing in spiritual wisdom and understanding produces three powerful benefits: our lives will honor and please God, we will produce fruit, and we will become better acquainted with the God who created us! Reflect on that for a moment.

Authentic Value

Recently, my oldest son wanted to sell one of his collector's cards on eBay. He assured me that it was worth "a *lot* of money!" I told him I wasn't sure if it was fake, and I was uncomfortable selling something I did not know much about. He continued to insist that it was real. He was so adamant about it that I began researching how to decipher if a card was fake or authentic. I discovered that if it was real, it could be worth between $400 and $700. One key to determining its authenticity was whether it had a thin black piece of card stock between the two regular-colored sides of the card. That would establish its worth. (The card did not end up being real, so it was not worth that amount.) Yet, strangely enough, even these markers were subjective. Markers became valuable based on what the consumer deemed as valuable. Thank God that His Word is nothing like a collector's card! Regardless of the consumers' opinions, God's Word never changes and never loses its value. It is not subject to the ever-changing evaluations of people. Instead, it stands firm throughout all generations as truth breathed by God. Such a truth is certainly worth our time, effort, and the surrender of our lives.

The value we give the pages between the covers of our Bibles will be evidenced not only in the time we spend in God's Word but also in how we live. We are exhorted to live "above reproach" (1 Timothy 3:2). The way we live is a huge indicator of whether or not we are heeding the words of Scripture. I love how Tim Challies defines the short phrase "above reproach." He writes,

What the ESV translates as "above reproach" is first a legal word that indicates a kind of innocence in the eyes of the law. It means that no one can legitimately rebuke you or make any charges against you that will stick. They may accuse, but your conduct will eventually acquit you by proving you blameless ("blameless" being a far more common translation than "above reproach"). Your life is so consistent that your reputation is credible, you are an example worth following, and you do not make the gospel look fake by teaching one thing while doing another. . . . The primary means through which you gain this characteristic is taking advantage of God's means of grace—reading the Bible and deliberately applying it, praying privately and with your family, faithfully attending your church's worship services, participating in the sacraments, and so on. These are the very means through which God extends his sanctifying grace and you cannot expect to be or remain above reproach if you neglect them.[2]

Application Leads to Worship

I have heard it said, "Worship is a response to God's revelation." The truth is that when we read His Word, learn more about Him, and apply Scripture to our lives, our hearts will be led to worship! In the book of Revelation, we are given a beautiful picture of what true worship looks like. In this beautiful picture of heaven, the doors are open for Jesus' disciple John to witness a celebration in eternity. There before him is a throne with a rainbow encircling it, a reminder of God's mercy on Noah's family during the Flood. Around the throne are twenty-four elders with crowns of gold on their heads. And there at the center of it all sits our God in all His majesty (see Revelation 4:1-6).

In a powerful and humble act acknowledging the One who is truly worthy, the elders cast their crowns before God. As the four living creatures erupt in worship before the throne, the twenty-four elders "fall down before Him who sits on the throne and worship Him who lives forever and ever, and cast their crowns before the throne, saying: 'You are worthy, O Lord'" (4:10-11, NKJV). The worthiness of God is so apparent to these elders that they erupt in a joyful noise and cast their crowns before the throne. I can only imagine what it would be like to be before God's throne and truly understand His absolute majesty and worthiness. Compared to the beauty and holiness of the King, these elders must feel a great sense of unworthiness. We are still here on earth, and our eyes are not yet able to witness the majesty of God, but God has provided His Word to us. The Bible is so full of wisdom and life and promise. It is a living book that waits to be applied, and if applied, it will lead us to a deep, reverent appreciation and love and worship of God.

Despite the elders' unworthiness, the crowns of life that they wear in heaven are such beautiful depictions of the place of grace in our lives. And as believers, we will all one day receive crowns in heaven. When we get there, we will understand the One who is truly worthy of worship. As a kid, I remember getting a paper crown whenever my family went to Burger King. I would be so upset when I lost my crown. Here on earth, we often vie for the equivalent of flimsy Burger King crowns, trying to grasp the glory that should be God's alone. Living with disordered desires and distorted agendas, we grasp at various things to signify our worth. On our heads we place people's admiration of us, our job, our role as a mother or wife. We try to bolster ourselves with these paper crowns. I can only imagine that when we get to heaven and are given a crown that really matters, we will finally comprehend the depths of our unworthiness before the King—and His worthiness will cause us to cast our crowns at His feet. It will suddenly be so clear that the paper Burger King crowns we threw tantrums over were temporary and insufficient.

But acknowledging God's worthiness is not just relegated to a future time in heaven. A response of true heart adoration can also be an act of worship here on earth. And what causes our hearts to fill up in worship of God? Learning more of who He is. As we get to know more about God—His provisions for us and His faithfulness—and as we allow Him to change our hearts through the application of His Word, we will grow to become more like Christ, and we will grow in our worship of Him. I have grown in my worship of God as I have grown in my love of God! As I get older, I become more and more aware of the ways that God has pursued me with His unfailing love. As my eyes have been opened to His chase, I have grown in my response toward Him—learning to love Him by obeying Him, praising Him, and submitting my life to Him over and over again. As I mentioned earlier, although I have pursued Him by studying His Word, I

I have grown in my worship of God as I have grown in my love of God!

have become more and more aware of how His love has chased me down, in and through His Word, which has then caused my heart to worship!

The Last Word

Application is the last step in the Inductive Bible Study process. But I want to point you toward another last. Jesus, revealed to us through the Bible, is the last Word. He is the final verdict—the last judgment or valuation. His sovereign hand is stretched over your life span. It's as if you were sentenced to death row—and then exonerated because of your innocence through Jesus' sacrificial death. He is the resting place for all your anxious thoughts and the redeemer of all the hopelessness you have experienced because of the chaos of sin.

"The last word" is a deeply ingrained American idiom that assumes whoever speaks last in an argument wins. In court cases, the prosecutor always gets to have the last word because the court system believes the prosecution holds the burden of proof. The beginning of Hebrews shows us that God spoke through His prophets in the Old Testament. But the last Word of all time is Jesus. As the writer of Hebrews says, "Long ago, at many times and in many ways, God spoke to our fathers by the prophets, but in these last days he has spoken to us by his Son, whom he appointed the heir of all things, through whom also he created the world. He is the radiance of the glory of God and the exact imprint of his nature, and he upholds the universe by the word of his power." (Hebrews 1:1-3, ESV).

Today you might feel that anxiety, loss, sickness, or barrenness have marked your life in a way you could never rewrite. You might feel that infertility has spoken its pain over you. Cancer might be the diagnosis that has clouded your vision and spoken death over your life. You might believe that your addiction has gone too far. But God spoke His permanent place of existence for you when He sent His Son, Jesus. We cannot deny what was indeed spoken over our lives two thousand years ago when Jesus defeated death once and for all. When we deny the Word's power in our lives, we deny Christ Himself—the fullness of His power. In the book of Matthew, Jesus says, "You are in error because you do not know the Scriptures or the power of God" (Matthew 22:29). The truth is, we all are in error if we do not believe what God says in His Word and come to a saving knowledge of Him.

Revelation includes these words from Jesus: "I am the Alpha and the Omega, the First and the Last, the Beginning and the End" (Revelation 22:13). Jesus "is before all things, and in him all things hold together" (Colossians 1:17). We know the end of the story: the last word wins! What a life we get to live when we submit to the wisdom of the Word of God as the last word or evaluation of our lives.

May we all be like Mary, who responded to the angel Gabriel like this: "I am the Lord's servant. . . . May it happen to me according to your word" (Luke 1:38, BSB). May we all have the humility to accept the truth, wisdom, and direction we find in God's Word. To settle into the application process, the final step of Inductive Bible Study is to say, like Mary, that we align ourselves with the truth of God's Word.

Conclusion

LEARNING A NEW SKILL can be extremely frustrating! As an adult, I need more time and mental energy to be a beginner at something. It is one thing to learn something new as a child, but it is humbling to take on new activities once you're grown up. You are an adult! Shouldn't this be easier? Recently, I started teaching myself how to hand-letter. I desired to learn this skill because I knew it would be great for making pictures for Instagram. On day two, though, I wanted to completely give up. I felt like I was in elementary school again. My first letters looked like chicken scratch, but as I continued to trace more letters, in a few weeks they began to get better and better. The learning curve was extremely frustrating, though. I went from just wanting to give up to pushing through how uncomfortable it made me feel.

Learning how to study the Bible in context is like developing any new skill. There are some hurdles to get over and insecurities to push through. Learn while you give yourself grace. And like all new things, it will eventually become second nature for you to ask questions of the text, research the historical context, look up words, and do the hard work of discovery. Eventually, you will think less and less about the process. Soon enough, you will do it without even trying. You will look into the context and dig just because it is less of a step-by-step process and more of an ebb and flow. It is like learning to ride a bike. When you first learned, you had to think about all the steps separately, but now you probably don't think about pedaling, braking, or turning—you do them instinctually. Once you walk yourself through a process multiple times, it becomes a natural part of you.

The Sword of the Spirit

A big new trend has taken over our area: axe throwing! My husband and I have gone one too many times. He is a natural. But me? While I can land an axe in the wood, let's just say that I'm not hitting any bull's-eyes. I find it a bit humorous that in the twenty-first century, a tool that was primarily used for cutting down trees, butchering animals, or as a weapon, has now been sized down for weekend entertainment where adults are munching food, chugging drinks, and laughing hysterically while throwing axes at a wall for a good time. Does that strike anyone else as odd? Okay . . . just me? An axe is a dangerous weapon that can seriously injure or kill someone, but we are using it to revitalize our date nights.

When we think about the sword of the Spirit in Ephesians 6, we know it represents the Word of God. But these days we think of a sword much as we do an axe: old-fashioned and mostly used for fun these days—maybe as part of a costume. The sword described in this passage, however, is not a pretend sword like a child might strap on for Halloween, nor like an axe we throw at the wall. The book of Ephesians compares God's Word to a real weapon— specifically a sword. "Put on the full armor of God, so that you can take your stand against the devil's schemes. . . . Take the helmet of salvation and the sword of the Spirit, which is the word of God"

(Ephesians 6:11, 17). Paul urges us to put on the armor of God so we will be ready when we are tested or when false teaching comes. When Paul wrote this passage, he probably had in mind the armor of a Roman soldier, which he would have been familiar with. I love how one commentary explains this passage:

> Paul's emphasis on armor, then, is not simply protection against the wicked spiritual forces that seek to bring down believers. The armor also testifies to the person's identity and loyalty. Jesus spoke of such loyalty in his call that believers acknowledge and confess him before others (Matt 10:32-33; Luke 12:8). Wearing the armor of God further distinguishes believers from those around them, as ones who seek holiness and justice, who practice kindness and forgiveness, and who humbly serve others above themselves. To draw a lighthearted analogy, as superfans wear clothing and hats with their team's insignia, so too wearing God's armor identifies believers as part of God's "team." Moreover, the virtues described serve to protect Paul's integrity in ministry. To the Corinthians he commends himself "in truthful speech and in the power of God; with weapons of righteousness in the right hand and in the left" (2 Corinthians 6:7). Paul invites the Romans to imagine themselves as actual "instruments" (the Greek term is the same) of righteousness, tools that God uses to further his kingdom (Romans 6:13).[1]

To use our sword (the Word of God) skillfully and with greatest effectiveness, we must be trained, skilled, and knowledgeable so we can use the Word both offensively and defensively against the enemy.

An Incredible Impact

The Word of God is powerful! Like many teens, I struggled with peer pressure and started to drift away from my daily Bible reading. I was in a challenging stage of life: I had just moved back to the United States from Thailand, and God's plan and ways seemed a bit cryptic to me. Having just left all my long-term friendships behind in Thailand, I struggled to feel like I belonged, and frankly, I was depressed.

Soon after returning to the US, I became a counselor at my grandparents' Christian day camp. One day, another camp counselor approached me and said, "I feel prompted to tell you this verse." She then proceeded to quote 1 Peter 5:7: "Cast all your anxiety on him because he cares for you." I remember that day like it was yesterday. God knew my heart, He knew my sadness, and He cared! *The God of the universe cared for me.* He cared for me in the state I was currently in: lonely, isolated, and experiencing all sorts of culture shock. That verse was exactly what I needed to hear, and it was powerful enough to send me back to reading God's Word. I returned to my bunk that night and scoured the pages of my Bible, underlining verse after verse and genuinely recommitting my life to Christ. My friends, God's Word is powerful and changes people's lives.

On a larger scale, consider the impact Scripture can have on a small minority group who have never had even one Bible verse in their language. There are a number of Bible translation organizations out there, and I had the privilege of growing up amid translators who worked for Wycliffe Bible Translators. The people group that my own parents worked with had never had God's Word in their language. Many of them loved God, but the only way for them to access His Word was to learn and understand a bigger people group's language that *did* have a translation of the

Bible in their language. Can you imagine? It would be like us having to learn French to be able to read and understand the Bible. As a result, people had to depend fully on their pastor as their only source of information about God and His Word. They were unable to study and learn from the Bible for themselves. Not surprisingly, non-Christians in this language group were uninterested because they did not want to learn a completely different language to know about "this God" that was being talked about.

Years later, when the Christians finally received the New Testament in their language—when they were finally able to read and understand it for themselves—they sang about it and told stories about it. It has become an integral part of their lives. Scripture's impact on their language resulted in worship services that included songs about how great it was to have the Bible! They began reading the Bible for themselves from beginning to end. More of them started attending church and asking their pastor questions about the text. The pastor was surprised that everyone was so curious. *So* many of them came to know Christ during this time. After they had the New Testament in their language, many of these believers emigrated to the United States and other countries to escape the civil war going on in their home country. As they began to understand God's Word, these young believers started returning to their war-torn country to share Christ with their own people.

What a powerful impact when you can picture Jesus in your own context!

These are results of being powerfully impacted by personal Bible reading. During the final read-through of the New Testament prior to printing, one lady said that when she read it, she could see Jesus through her language, and she could see Him sweating in her village and dwelling amid her people group. What a powerful impact when you *can picture Jesus in your own context*!

As John Piper writes, God's Word will always change people's lives:

> Story after story shows that the Word of God has life giving power. Phaitoon Hathamart described to us how it was Matthew 11:28-30 that gave him Christian life when he was a Buddhist. St. Augustine said it was Romans 13:13 that stunned him into life. For Martin Luther it was Romans 1:16. For Jonathan Edwards it was 1 Timothy 1:17. And for the murderer Tokichi Ishii, who was converted just before his execution in Japan in 1918, it was the simple word, "Father, forgive them, for they know not what they do." He said, "I was stabbed to the heart, as if by a five-inch nail."[2]

Pass It Along

My husband and I had an extremely eventful honeymoon, as in my husband almost died. I have read enough news stories where honeymooners go off to their favorite resort, tragedy strikes, and one of them ends up killed. During a day of deep-sea diving in Fiji, we came close to being one of those stories.

My husband and I both love to travel, and it didn't take much to convince us that we would never regret taking a month-long honeymoon. Sounds exorbitant, I know, but you will never be freer than when you are first married. So off we went on our grand adventure—first to New Zealand, then Fiji, and finally driving the coast of California!

When we arrived in Fiji, we were intent on one experience: scuba diving! We are both avid adventurists, and it seemed like the perfect time to get scuba certified. We found an outlet that could certify, and we told the instructor that neither of us had ever scuba dived (except for ten years prior) and we wanted to get our license so we could dive all around the world.

The instructor agreed, and he told us to meet back at this same spot in the morning. The next morning, bright and early, he told us to hop on the boat with the rest of the group and get geared up.

I looked at my husband. "Aren't we going to get trained first? Don't you feel like we should learn the basics?"

My husband, with his normal can-do attitude, brushed it off. "Let's just do what he says. He knows he's training us!"

Once we got on the boat, we made our way out to sea, and the instructor told us all to get our tanks on! I panicked. *How do you clear your mask?* I thought to myself. *What are the rules again?* I was about twelve years old the one and only time I had previously scuba dived. *What are the hand signals?* We looked at the Australian divers in front of us and confessed that we had only been diving once.

Overhearing us, the instructor laughed. "Oh, I thought you wanted to get *deep-water* certified. These are all scuba diving instructors, and they are doing their deep dives today."

"No! We want to just get certified—not deep-water certified!"

"Well, come with us. We will take care of you, just follow our lead. You are already on the boat!"

We naively chose to jump in and follow along that day. As we dove deeper and deeper, the water was so clear, so beautiful. We dove along a cliff-like coral structure in the ocean. Moray eels were poking out of the holes, and the fish were unbelievable. I couldn't believe the things I was seeing! The deeper we went, the more it felt like a world undiscovered. It was as if I were peeling back layers of amazing sights that most people would never get to see in their lifetime. I was definitely convinced I needed to get trained in how to scuba dive.

The next day, on a high from the previous dive, I was ready

for training. We learned all the basics: how to put your gear on, how to clear your mask, and what each hand signal meant. I practiced giving my husband my extra air if his air were to run out in an emergency underwater, and we talked about why we need to slowly come to the surface, waiting around fifteen feet under for three to five minutes so we wouldn't get air bubbles in our blood. I was in my element. We were going to do more dives and see amazing sights under the surface of the ocean, and now I had the confidence to do it. We were ready!

After our training was completed, we were ready to do a shipwreck dive where we would literally explore a sunken ship. We were diving with a few other strangers, and once again we made our way out into the waters. As we dove deeper, we swam farther and farther away from the boat. We explored, taking in all the beautiful fish. Eventually, we arrived at the sunken ship. I motioned to my husband to check his air. He looked at me panicked—he was almost out of air, and so was another guy in our group. I quickly swam over to the instructor and motioned toward my husband.

"He is almost out of air!" I tapped my air valve.

He motioned back to show us that we should chill out and have fun.

We once again began to follow the instructor, and soon we were inside the shipwreck. I saw the panicked look on both my husband's and the other guy's face. About that time, we came upon a *huge* puffer fish! It was floating in the middle of the shipwreck. As much as I wanted to continue looking at it, I knew we had to get back to the boat. So I left and motioned for my husband to follow. The other guy was hot on our tail. We started making our way back to the boat by ourselves. Looking through the murky water, I was feeling anxious, and I glanced sideways at my new husband. All of a sudden, his eyes got big like the puffer fish. I grabbed his air valve and saw it said zero. Like the trained scuba diver that I had just become, I grabbed my extra mouthpiece and stuck it into his mouth. At that exact moment, the instructor caught up with us and did the same thing to the guy behind me. Whew! I saw his face relax. Nothing like being able to breathe again. Shoulder to shoulder, we made our way back to the boat and were forever grateful that this story did not have a different ending!

Deep-diving into the pages of Scripture is a lot like scuba diving. It doesn't just benefit you to be trained; it also benefits others! You can plumb the depths of the pages of Scripture, and if you take the time, you will inevitably see things that many others will not notice. Likewise, if you only skim Scripture passages without learning how to study them, you will overlook so much that God wants to share with you and others. Don't miss such a wonderful opportunity!

I truly believe that utilizing the Bible study tools in this book will not just bring new meaning to *your* life but also will be a means by which you are able to share with others what you have learned. The Bible describes Scripture as "God-breathed," so when you are reading it, you are reading the words of God Himself. Consider that! It's amazing that we can literally read the words of the God who created us! And when you pass on to others tools to study the Word, you are sharing God's breath with them. You are giving them *life*. If you are trained in Inductive Bible Study methods, you will become an encouragement to others as you share what God is teaching you. You can pass along that teaching with confidence, exhorting them toward godly living.

Learning how to scuba dive was not rocket science. It wasn't so difficult that only certain people could grasp the rules and regulations. It just meant learning and following a number of key guidelines. Likewise, Scripture reading is not reserved for those who seem smarter or have more education. With a little effort, you will come to the conclusion, *Hey, understanding the Bible is not as difficult as I thought.* God meant for His Word to be understood. And what is truly amazing is that the Bible equates understanding the Scriptures with life itself. The Bible is like air to the living, breathing soul. As God says in the book of Amos, "Seek me and live" (5:4). If we want to live, well, it's easy: we must seek God. The Scriptures are a means to an end: the pathway to knowing and loving God. With just a little bit of training and practice, we can grow in confidence to explore deeper waters, to speak about God's revelation with intention and purpose. In 1 Peter 2:2, we read, "Like newborn babies, crave pure spiritual milk, so that by it you may grow up in your salvation." We grow through reading the Word of God. As we grow in understanding God's Word, we can begin using the Scriptures to exhort and encourage our spouse, children, and friends.

My hope for you when you close this book is that you will be inspired to learn to study God's Word—and that you will also desire to share your love for studying God's Word with others! I hope that you experience the joy of studying the Bible in its cultural and historical context, and that it will bring clarity and excitement to your Scripture reading! As you begin to chase sacred, my hope is that you will get excited to open the pages of the Bible every single day—and that you will yearn to hear from God and grow in your love of Him. And finally, my hope is that you will experience how personal and intimate God's Word is: words so relevant and directly applicable to your heart and life that you wonder how you could live without them. May you learn to lean into His love through the pages of Scripture and experience what it is to have a relationship with the King of kings. Remember, you might feel like you are opening the Bible to chase Him, but you will soon realize that all along He has been chasing you.

God meant for His Word to be understood.

BIBLE STUDY RESOURCES

THERE ARE A TON OF COMMENTARIES and study resources out there, so it's easy to feel overwhelmed when you go searching for one. That's why I'm including these lists of some of my favorite Bible study resources: commentaries, videos, websites, and more. Give them a try to see which ones work best for you!

Commentaries

- The NIV Application Commentary
- Understanding the Bible Commentary Series
- The New American Commentary
- Tyndale Old Testament Commentaries
- Tyndale New Testament Commentaries
- The New International Commentary on the New Testament
- The IVP Bible Dictionary Series
- Word Biblical Commentary

Resources for Historical and Cultural Context

- *Rose Book of Bible Charts, Maps, and Time Lines*
- *God's Bible Timeline: The Big Book of Biblical History*

Study Bibles

- *The New Inductive Study Bible* (NASB)
- *Holy Land Illustrated Bible* (CSB)
- *NIV Life Application Study Bible*
- *ESV Gospel Transformation Study Bible*

Other Study Resources

- BibleProject videos, available for free online (bibleproject .com/explore): I use these to get an overview of each book of the Bible before I start studying it.
- Logos Bible Software: I use this software for a lot of my studying, including word studies. A basic package includes multiple Bible versions and several Bible study resources, such as commentaries, encyclopedias, dictionaries, devotionals, and more.
- Blue Letter Bible (blueletterbible.org)

The following resources are great if you're not familiar with Greek and Hebrew:

- *New International Dictionary of Old Testament Theology and Exegesis*
- *The Enhanced Brown-Driver-Briggs Hebrew and English Lexicon*
- Bible Hub (biblehub.com)

Word Study Resources

Bible Hub and Blue Letter Bible are excellent online resources for word studies. Below, we'll walk through how to do a word study at both these sites. We'll focus on the word *trial* in James 1:2: "Consider it pure joy, my brothers and sisters, whenever you face *trials* of many kinds" (emphasis added).

Bible Hub

Biblehub.com is extremely straightforward to use for a word study. I learned how to use this website from Amy Gannett, a friend of mine who runs an online ministry and a company called Tiny Theologians.

First, search for James 1:2. The search will show the verse in many different translations. Scroll down and check out all the ways scholars have translated *trial* into English, including *test* and *temptation.*

Next, click the "Interlin" (interlinear) tab toward the top of the screen. This will bring up the passage in Greek, and above the word you are choosing to study you will see a Strong's Concordance number. For the word *trial*, the number is 3986 (e).

When you click the number, it will bring up all the passages in the Bible that include the word *trials.* Then you can read all the ways the Greek word is used in Scripture, along with all its possible meanings!

Then scroll through all the verses that use this word. I want you to pay close attention to how different translators use a number of English words for the same Greek word. This plainly shows that we might not have a single English word that embodies all the meanings of this Greek term. The English translation of a word might also be different depending on the context and the part of speech.

Blue Letter Bible

At blueletterbible.org, search for James 1:2 again. (You can choose from many Bible versions; in this example, I selected NIV from the drop-down menu.)

Note that all the verses of James 1 appear in a list. Click on "Tools" to the left of James 1:2, and then click on the "Interlinear" tab (if it didn't come up automatically).

Next, scroll down and click the Strong's number next to *trials*, which is G3986.

In the Strong's Definitions section, you will see this definition on the screen: "a putting to proof (by experiment (of good), experience (of evil), solicitation, discipline or provocation); by implication, adversity:—temptation, try" (https://www.blueletterbible .org/lexicon/g3986/nlt/mgnt/0-1/).

Then you can read all the Scripture verses that use that same Greek word. In this way, you will be able to determine the semantic range (see chapter 11) and the context.

Acknowledgments

FIRST OFF, I WANT TO THANK THE LORD, who strengthened me during one of the hardest seasons of my life. He has always been faithful, and He saw this work through to the very shaky end. You are a God with open arms to me, a God who has comforted me, guided me, and spoken so many truths to my heart. God, this book is, first and foremost, for Your honor and Your glory. Your love is indescribable.

Most importantly, to my family. Mom and Dad, you have been my safe haven, the most involved out of anyone, and the backbone of support I needed. I couldn't have written this book without you. Mom, I cannot count the hours you pored over this book or the many conversations and phone calls you took to see this work through. Without a shadow of a doubt, I see your selfless love as an outpouring of the Lord's continual work in your life. You cared for my children, boosted my spirits, and diligently read and revisited chapters alongside me. This book would not have happened without you flying up to help me! Dad, you also spent countless hours looking over this book with your edits. You championed me, encouraged me, and took every phone call willingly. You guys are the best parents in the world. I cannot envision more supportive and loving parents. You guys have more integrity than anyone I know, and your unwavering desire to see God glorified and your consistent encouragement are unmatched. Briana and Dad, thank you for your initial edits; both of you have such a gift. I could not have done this without my family. JB, thanks for always being so proud of me and asking me questions! It never goes unnoticed. Thank you to my husband for standing alongside me in all of this. Jamie, I love you.

And to my children—Paxton, Barkley, Hudson, Copley, and Tatum—you are the center of my universe. Your love is boundless. You are not just my biggest cheerleaders, but the very reason I live and breathe. You love to ask me questions about my writing, and you have such soft hearts. All of you are great at taking an interest in others and sharing about the Lord, and your hearts are pure gold. You guys were the best decision I ever made. Thank you for unknowingly supporting me all this time.

Memere, Nana, and Poppy, you built a legacy that I got to step into. Your prayers have brought me forward, of that I am sure! Mama Kathy V. D., I am always endlessly thankful for your prayers and the way you fight endlessly for my family on your knees!

On a more personal note, I could not have achieved this without my prayer partners: Alyson Griffin, Amy Holombo, Stephanie Wilcox, Cait Aho, and Jamie Moody. Your steadfast love during this writing season was unparalleled. The timely texts and messages moved this project forward. Alyson, for the ways you have literally picked me up off the ground, thank you. Stephanie Wilcox, there is no one more gifted in standing alongside the suffering—thank you. Amy Holombo, you are such a gifted encourager. Alyson and Cait, for purchasing every product—I'm forever thankful. Ashley Van Dyke, there were quite a few times you took my kids and I got a quiet house to write—thank you! Chelsea Van Dyke, thank you for showing an interest in my work! Josh Van Dyke and Erjona Van Dyke, thank you for all the questions, interest, and love! Special thanks to my pastoral team, Jordan and Jamie Moody. Jamie, not only were you a supportive prayer partner, but you were also invaluable in reviewing this book, discussing it with me, and aiding in the development of specific chapters. Jordan, this would not be possible without you and your wife! Thank you for your edits and for meeting with me. I am eternally grateful to both of you.

To Hope Fellowship, a church that took a chance on me. I cry about the love and support my church family has shown me! Undeserved love! My church body has lifted me up over and over again and supported me in countless ways.

To everyone at Tyndale, you took a chance on me as a first-time author, and I will always be thankful for that. I have only had an amazing experience with you all! You guys love your work, and it shows. Kara Leonino, your diligence, support, and talent have been foundational to this work. We were instant friends, and I love how vulnerable and real you are! God has great, amazing things for you. To my incredible editors, Danika Kelly and Stephanie Rische: your combined skills and encouragement are unparalleled. I'm truly fortunate to benefit from your expertise and dedication in making this project shine at its brightest. Danika, you are SO gifted and talented. I am so thankful for all your kind words and your ability to catch the details and always make things sound more gracious.

To my agent, Debbie Alsdorf, you are the perfect agent for me. So supportive and kind! You have encouraged me so much throughout this process.

To my Chasing Sacred team: Stephanie Wilcox, God knew when He brought you alongside me. WOW, it is the biggest gift.

Thank you for standing with me all these years. Emilee, Brooke, Maggie, Kate, Audrey, and Stephanie E.—you all have impacted me in so many ways. Thank you for taking on the mission of Chasing Sacred!

I know that I am missing people who deserve to be acknowledged, so thank you to anyone and everyone who has prayed for me as I wrote this book.

Do I hope the inductive method of studying will guide you in your personal study and make the Word come alive to you? Yes! I am certainly not the first person who has introduced the Inductive Bible Study as a method of great help in studying God's Word. Robert A. Traina and Irving Jensen, who developed an inductive approach to God's Word, and Kay Arthur, who spent many years creating biblical resources through Precept Ministries, were all adherents of the inductive method. While writing this book, I relied heavily on my hermeneutics class at Regent University— thank you, Professor Dwight Sheets. I also want to thank Douglas Stuart and Gordon D. Fee for writing their book *How to Read the Bible for All Its Worth* and Jen Wilkin for exciting a generation of women to love God's Word through her book *Women of the Word*.

Notes

INTRODUCTION

1. Maria Baer, "Why There Are So Many 'Miraculous' Stories of Bibles Surviving Disaster," *Christianity Today*, December 21, 2020, https://www.christianitytoday.com/ct/2021/january-february/bible-survival-flood-fire-disaster-miracle-faith.html.

2. John Mark Comer, *The Ruthless Elimination of Hurry* (Colorado Springs, CO: WaterBrook, 2019), 39.

CHAPTER 1: FIND SOMETHING WORTH CHASING AFTER

1. Richard Alan Fuhr Jr. and Andreas J. Köstenberger, *Inductive Bible Study: Observation, Interpretation, and Application through the Lenses of History, Literature, and Theology* (Nashville: B&H Academic, 2016), 20.

2. Martin Luther, *Lectures on Romans*, The Library of Christian Classics, trans. and ed. Wilhelm Pauck (Philadelphia, PA: Westminster, 1961), 15:128, quoted in *Evangelicals Engaging Emergent*, ed. William D. Henard and Adam W. Greenway (Nashville: B&H Academic, 2009), 34.

CHAPTER 2: EXPERIENCE THE DELIGHT OF GOD'S WORD

1. Daniel L. Aiken, "Delight," Bible Study Tools, accessed September 23, 2023, https://www.biblestudytools.com/dictionary/delight.

2. C. Claiborne Ray, "Q & A; Hillside Trees," *New York Times*, March 13, 2001, https://www.nytimes.com/2001/03/13/science/q-a-hillside-trees.html.

3. Alfred, Lord Tennyson, "The Grandmother," st. 8, lines 3–4, Poeticous, accessed September 23, 2023, https://www.poeticous.com/tennyson/the-grandmother.

CHAPTER 3: DISCOVER THE BIGGER STORY OF THE BIBLE

1. Encyclopedia.com, s.v. "theme," last updated June 27, 2018, https://www
.encyclopedia.com/literature-and-arts/performing-arts/music-history/theme.

2. "5 Things Bible Scholars Mean When They Use the Term 'Biblical
Theology,'" Zondervan.com, accessed September 24, 2023, https://www
.zondervan.com/p/biblical-theology/five-ways/. Adapted from Edward
W. Klink III and Darian R. Lockett, *Understanding Biblical Theology: A
Comparison of Theory and Practice* (Grand Rapids, MI: Zondervan, 2012).

3. Brian Tabb, "Rejoice Even Though: Facing the Challenges to Joy,"
Desiring God, October 16, 2016, https://www.desiringgod.org/articles
/rejoice-even-though/.

4. Dictionary.com, s.v. "typify (*v.*)," accessed August 29, 2023, https://
www.dictionary.com/browse/typify.

5. *ESV Gospel Transformation Study Bible* (Wheaton, IL: Crossway, 2019),
introduction.

CHAPTER 4: RECOGNIZE FALSE TEACHING

1. Gordon D. Fee and Douglas Stuart, *How to Read the Bible for All Its Worth*,
4th ed. (Grand Rapids, MI: Zondervan, 2014), 119.

2. Fee and Stuart, 124.

3. Alec Motyer, "What Is Progressive Revelation?" Crossway, May 26, 2018,
https://www.crossway.org/articles/what-is-progressive-revelation/.

4. Eduardo Medina, "Mehran Karimi Nasseri, Who Inspired 'The Terminal,'
Dies in Paris Airport," *New York Times,* November 13, 2022, https://www
.nytimes.com/2022/11/13/world/europe/mehran-karimi-nasseri-dead.html.

5. Robert N. Wilkin, "New Testament Repentance: Repentance in the Gospels
and Acts," Bible.org, August 30, 2004, https://bible.org/seriespage/4-new
-testament-repentance-repentance-gospels-and-acts.

CHAPTER 5: THE ROLE OF THE SPIRIT

1. Randy Alcorn, "The Relationship between the Holy Spirit and the Word of
God," Eternal Perspective Ministries, February 25, 2010, https://www.epm
.org/resources/2010/Feb/25/relationship-between-holy-spirit-and-word-god.

2. Alcorn.

3. R. C. Sproul, *Knowing Scripture*, rev. ed. (Downers Grove, IL: IVP Books,
2009), 70.

4. James Daugherty, *The Landing of the Pilgrims*, Landmark Books (New York:
Random House, 1981), 38.

5. Merriam-Webster Dictionary Online, *s.v. "infallible" and s.v. "inerrant,"
accessed November 27, 2023,* https://www.merriam-webster.com/dictionary
/infallible; *https://www.merriam-webster.com/dictionary/inerrant.*

6. "Who Wrote Most of the New Testament?," Got Questions, last updated

March 30, 2022, https://www.gotquestions.org/who-wrote-most-of-the
-New-Testament.html.

7. *Baker's Evangelical Dictionary of Biblical Theology*, s.v. "amen," https://
www.biblestudytools.com/dictionary/amen/; "Biblical Trust Isn't Blind,"
BibleProject, November 9, 2020, podcast episode, https://bibleproject
.com/podcast/biblical-trust-isnt-blind/.

8. R. C. Sproul, "What Does 'Amen' Mean?," Ligonier Ministries, April 5,
2019, https://www.ligonier.org/learn/articles/what-does-word-amen-mean.

CHAPTER 6: THE ROLE OF PRAYER

1. Paul E. Miller, *A Praying Life: Connecting with God in a Distracting World*
(Colorado Springs, CO: NavPress, 2017), 37.

2. "James 1:26-27 Commentary," updated October 12, 2019, Precept Austin,
https://www.preceptaustin.org/james_126-27.

CHAPTER 8: OBSERVE AND ASK

1. "Gathering Apples," Bible.org, accessed September 28, 2023, https://
bible.org/illustration/gathering-apples.

2. Jen Wilkin, *Women of the Word: How to Study the Bible with Both Our
Hearts and Our Minds*, 2nd ed. (Wheaton, IL: Crossway, 2019), 67.

3. Mark L. Strauss, "Mark: The Gospel of the Servant-Messiah: The
Once-Neglected Gospel," BibleProject, accessed September 29, 2023,
https://bibleproject.com/articles/mark-gospel-servant-messiah.

4. Richard Alan Fuhr Jr. and Andreas J. Köstenberger, *Inductive Bible Study:
Observation, Interpretation, and Application through the Lenses of History,
Literature, and Theology* (Nashville: B&H Academic, 2016), 76.

5. Fuhr and Köstenberger, 74.

CHAPTER 9: UNCOVER CONTEXT

1. Gregory Koukl, *Street Smarts: Using Questions to Answer Christianity's
Toughest Challenges* (Grand Rapids, MI: Zondervan, 2023), 187.

2. Robert H. Stein, *A Basic Guide to Interpreting the Bible: Playing by the
Rules*, 2nd ed. (Grand Rapids, MI: Baker Academic, 2011), 53.

3. Jen Wilkin, *Women of the Word: How to Study the Bible with Both Our
Hearts and Our Minds*, 2nd ed. (Wheaton, IL: Crossway, 2019), 35.

4. Wilkin, 66.

5. E. Randolph Richards and Brandon J. O'Brien, *Misreading Scripture with
Western Eyes: Removing Cultural Blinders to Better Understand the Bible*
(Downers Grove, IL: IVP, 2012), 97.

6. E. Randolph Richards and Richard James, *Misreading Scripture with
Individualist Eyes: Patronage, Honor, and Shame in the Biblical World*
(Downers Grove, IL: IVP, 2020), 12.

7. R. C. Sproul, *Knowing Scripture*, rev. ed. (Downers Grove, IL: IVP Books, 2009), 118.

8. *ESV Gospel Transformation Study Bible* (Wheaton, IL: Crossway, 2019), study note on Ephesians 1:3-10.

CHAPTER 10: IDENTIFY GENRE

1. Kristie Anyabwile, *Literarily: How Understanding Bible Genres Transforms Bible Study* (Chicago, IL: Moody Publishers, 2022), 45.

2. Robert H. Stein, *A Basic Guide to Interpreting the Bible: Playing by the Rules*, 2nd ed. (Grand Rapids, MI: Baker Academic, 2011), 108.

3. Stein, *Basic Guide to Interpreting the Bible*, 79.

4. "Background and Introduction to Esther," Grace Online Library, accessed October 13, 2023, https://graceonlinelibrary.org/blog/background -introduction-to-esther.

5. Joe Linares, *Proclaiming God's Stories: How to Preach Old Testament Historical Narrative* (Greenville, SC: Bob Jones University Press, 2009), 37–38.

6. Adele Berlin, quoted in Linares, 58.

7. Encyclopedia.com, s.v. "principle (*n.*)," from *The Oxford Pocket Dictionary of Current English*, updated May 23, 2018, https://www.encyclopedia .com/social-sciences-and-law/law/law/principle.

8. Linares, *Proclaiming God's Stories*, 47–48.

9. Gordon D. Fee and Douglas Stuart, *How to Read the Bible for All Its Worth*, 4th ed. (Grand Rapids, MI: Zondervan , 2014), 233.

10. Fee and Stuart, 240.

11. Stein, *Basic Guide to Interpreting the Bible*, 133.

12. A. Berkeley Mickelsen and Alvera M. Mickelsen, *Understanding Scripture: How to Read and Study the Bible*, rev. ed. (Peabody, MA: Hendrickson, 1992), 86.

13. Fee and Stuart, *How to Read the Bible*, 192.

14. Bridget Grenville-Cleave, Ilona Boniwell, and Tina B. Tessina, *The Happiness Equation: 100 Factors That Can Add To or Subtract From Your Happiness* (New York: Adams Media, 2008), 104.

15. Richard A. Burridge, "Biography, Ancient," in *Dictionary of New Testament Background: A Compendium of Contemporary Biblical Scholarship*, ed. Craig A. Evans and Stanley E. Porter (Downers Grove, IL: InterVarsity Press, 2000), 168.

16. I learned about interpreting the Gospels horizontally and vertically from Fee and Stuart, *How to Read the Bible for All Its Worth*, 140–146.

17. R. C. Sproul, *Knowing Scripture*, rev. ed. (Downers Grove, IL: IVP Books, 2009), 76.

18. Lynn H. Cohick, *The Gospels as the Story of Jesus*, Bible Survey Video Series (Bellingham, WA: Lexham Press, 2021).

19. Fee and Stuart, *How to Read the Bible*, 82.
20. Fee and Stuart, 84.
21. *Apocalyptic* comes from the Greek word *apokalypsis*. See Blue Letter Bible, s.v. "apokalypsis (n.)," accessed October 15, 2023, https://www.blueletterbible .org/lexicon/g602/kjv/tr/0-1/.
22. Mickelsen and Mickelsen, *Understanding Scripture*, 112.
23. Mickelsen and Mickelsen, 105.
24. Mickelsen and Mickelsen, 22.

CHAPTER 11: INTERPRET

1. Julia B. Higgins, *Empowered and Equipped: Bible Exposition for Women Who Teach the Scriptures* (Nashville: B&H Academic, 2022), 116.
2. A. Berkeley Mickelsen and Alvera M. Mickelsen, *Understanding Scripture: How to Read and Study the Bible*, rev. ed. (Peabody, MA: Hendrickson, 1992), 56.
3. James E. Smith, *The Old Testament Books Made Simple* (Joplin, MO: College Press, 2009), 24–25.

CHAPTER 12: APPLY

1. Richard Alan Fuhr Jr. and Andreas J. Köstenberger, *Inductive Bible Study: Observation, Interpretation, and Application through the Lenses of History, Literature, and Theology* (Nashville: B&H Academic, 2016), 316.
2. Tim Challies, "The Character of the Christian: Above Reproach," Challies .com, January 21, 2016, https://www.challies.com/articles/the-character -of-the-christian-above-reproach.

CONCLUSION

1. Lynn H. Cohick, *The Letter to the Ephesians*, The New International Commentary on the New Testament (Grand Rapids, MI: Eerdmans, 2020), 417.
2. John Piper, "Sweeter than Honey, Better than Gold," Desiring God, January 6, 1991, https://www.desiringgod.org/messages/sweeter-than -honey-better-than-gold.

About the Author

MIKELLA VAN DYKE is a wife, mother, and the founder of Chasing Sacred, a ministry that provides resources to help women study the Bible and grow closer to God. What began as a devotional blog became an organization with a team of writers who produce theologically rich Bible study resources. She has a master's in practical theology from Regent University, where she fell deeply in love with the process of hermeneutics and wanted to share her knowledge and love of the Word with others. She coleads Bible studies at her local church and enjoys speaking and sharing God's Word at conferences and retreats. She and her husband, Jamie, live in New Hampshire with their five kids, and she's often found riding a four-wheeler or reading the Bible with them.

CHASING SACRED

Teaching Women How to Study the Bible

Bible Studies
Journals
E-courses
Blog
& More

WE EQUIP WOMEN
WITH SOUND THEOLOGY AND DOCTRINE
TO PROPERLY READ, INTERPRET, AND
APPLY THE TEACHING OF THE BIBLE.

Follow us on Instagram

@chasingsacred

Visit our Website

ChasingSacred.com

Life Transformation through Bible Translation

Did you know there are more than 7,000 languages in the world? Unfortunately, about 1,200 of those language communities—representing approximately 100 million people—do not have a single verse of Scripture in words they best understand. Seed Company is a Bible translation organization working to change that.

Believing the Bible is living, active, and relevant for all people, in all cultures, for all time (Hebrews 4:12; 2 Timothy 3:16; 1 Peter 1:23-25), Seed Company partners with other translation organizations and translators—local to their own communities—to see God's Word transforming lives, in every language, in this generation. When people have access to Scripture in the words they think in and dream in, they finally understand that God knows them and loves them.

Just ask Pedro. This 66-year-old speaker of a lesser-known language in South America has attended several Bible translation workshops where Scripture is being translated for his community. Not only has his understanding of God's Word increased, but he longs to teach gospel truth to the next generation. He joyfully reports, "I understand that we do not worship a dead God, but a living and great God." Seed Company is grateful to be working in more than 900 languages to see others like Pedro embracing the hope and truth of Scripture.

Learn more at seedcompany.com

 Seed Company

Photography by Grant Daniels

CP1979

Join Mikella Van Dyke as she unpacks what it truly means to chase after God.

In *Chasing Sacred*, Mikella Van Dyke breaks down the misconceptions and reservations so many of us have about what it means to study the Bible and helps readers learn a practical, step-by-step approach to understanding God's Word.

In the *Chasing Sacred Bible Study*, Mikella will help you unpack God's Word in a new way, using the Inductive Bible Study method to teach a systematic, empowering approach.

Accompanying streaming video available at TyndaleChristianResources.com.